The Farmer Boy and How He Became Commander-in-Chief

Morrison Heady

Edited by William M. Thayer

ESPRIOS.COM
ESPRIOS DIGITAL PUBLISHING

THE

FARMER BOY,

AND

HOW HE BECAME COMMANDER-IN-CHIEF.

BY UNCLE JUVINELL.

EDITED BY
WILLIAM M. THAYER,
AUTHOR OF "THE PIONEER BOY," ETC.

SEVENTH THOUSAND.

1864.

INTRODUCTION.

BY REV. WILLIAM M. THAYER.

The reader will remember, that, in the preface of "THE PRINTER BOY," I promised the next volume should be "THE FARMER BOY; OR, HOW GEORGE WASHINGTON BECAME PRESIDENT." That pledge has never been redeemed, though some labor has been performed with reference to it. And now Providence seems to direct the fulfilment of the promise by the pen of another, soon to be well known, I doubt not, to thousands of young readers;—"Uncle Juvinell."

The advance sheets of a volume from his pen, upon the early life of Washington, have been placed in my hands for examination. I have carefully perused the work, and find it to be of so high a character, and so well adapted to the exigencies of the times, that I voluntarily abandon the idea of preparing the proposed volume myself, and most cordially recommend this work to the youth of our beloved land. I take this step with all the more readiness, when I learn that the author has persevered in his labors, though totally blind and almost deaf; and I gladly transfer the title which I proposed to give my own book to his excellent work, well satisfied that the act will prove a public benefit.

The reader will find that Mr. Heady (Uncle Juvinell) has produced a very entertaining and instructive volume. It is written in a racy, sprightly style, that cannot fail to captivate the mind. Partaking himself of the buoyancy and good humor of boyhood, the author is able to write for the boys in a manner that is at once attractive and profitable. He has written a live book of one, who, "though dead, yet speaketh." It is replete with facts, and lessons of wisdom. The virtues are taught both by precept and example, and the vices are held up in all their deformity to warn and save. Religion, too, receives its just tribute, and wears the crown of glory.

The appearance of this volume is timely. Adapted as it is to magnify the patriotic virtues, and the priceless worth of the government under which we live, it will prove a valuable contribution to the juvenile literature of the land. In this period of mighty struggles and issues, when our nation is groaning and travailing in pain to bring forth a future of surpassing renown and grandeur, it is important to inspire the hearts of American youth by the noblest examples of patriotism and virtue. And such is WASHINGTON, the "Father of his Country." It is best that the young of this battling age should study his character and emulate his deeds. His life was the richest legacy that he could leave to unborn generations, save the glorious Republic that he founded; and well will it be for the youth of our country when that life becomes to them the stimulus to exalted aims. Then loyalty will be free as air, and rebellions be unknown; then treason will hide its hydra-head, and our insulted flag wave in triumph where the last chain of slavery is broken.

This volume will do its part to hasten this consummation of our patriot-hopes. Over its pleasant pages, then, we extend the right hand of fellowship to its author, though a stranger to us. Long may his able pen hold out! Widely may this his last work circulate! Blessed may be the fruits!

W. M. T.

FRANKLIN, MASS., October, 1863.

PREFACE.

Our beloved country, my dear young readers, has passed through one great revolution; and it is now in the midst of another, which promises to prove even more momentous in its consequences.

Knowing, therefore, the deep and lasting impression the great events of the day must needs produce upon your opening minds, the author of this book has been casting about him how he might contribute to your and the nation's good. As he is altogether bereft of sight, and nearly so of hearing, he is, of course, unable to lift a hand in his country's defence, or raise his voice in her justification. But she has a future; and for that he entertains an earnest hope, that through you, the rising generation, he may do something.

To this end, therefore, he has written this volume, wherein he has endeavored to set forth, in a manner more calculated to attract and impress the youthful mind than has perhaps been heretofore attempted, the life and character of our good and great George Washington.

By so doing, he hopes to awaken in your minds a desire to imitate the example and emulate the virtues of this greatest and wisest of Americans. For should he succeed in this, and thereby influence a thousand of you, when arrived at man's estate, to remain loyal to your country in her hour of peril (who might else have been tempted to turn their hand against her), then shall his humble pen have done more for her future welfare than he could have done for her present deliverance, had he the wielding of a thousand swords.

And, should he ever have reason to suppose that such were really the case, far happier would he be, even in the dark and silent depths of his solitude, than the renowned victor of a hundred battle-fields, in all the blaze and noise of popular applause. Hoping that this little book may, for your sakes, fulfil the object for which it was written, and prove but the beginning of a long and pleasant acquaintance, he will conclude by begging to subscribe himself your true friend and well-wisher,

MORRISON HEADY.

ELK CREEK, SPENCER COUNTY, KY., 1863.

CONTENTS.

Introduction

WHEREIN IT WILL APPEAR WHO UNCLE JUVINELL IS, AND HOW HE CAME TO WRITE THE LIFE OF "THE FARMER BOY" FOR THE LITTLE FOLKS.

I.

George at School,

IN WHICH THE YOUNG READER WILL FIND SOME ACCOUNT OF THE BIRTH, CHILDHOOD, AND EARLY EDUCATION OF GEORGE WASHINGTON, AND THE STORY OF HIS LITTLE HATCHET; FROM WHICH HE MAY DRAW A WHOLESOME MORAL, IF HE BE DESIROUS OF GROWING IN VIRTUE; TOGETHER WITH OTHER MATTERS OF INTEREST AND IMPORTANCE HARDLY TO BE FOUND ELSEWHERE.

II.

The First Sorrow

SHOWING HOW GEORGE MET WITH THE FIRST GREAT SORROW OF HIS LIFE IN THE DEATH OF HIS FATHER; AND HOW HIS MOTHER WAS LEFT A YOUNG WIDOW, WITH THE CARE OF A LARGE FAMILY; WITH SOME REMARKS ON THE PRUDENCE AND WISDOM SUE DISPLAYED IN THE REARING OF HER CHILDREN; TOGETHER WITH THE STORY OF THE SORREL COLT, WHICH UNCLE JUVINELL INTRODUCES BY WAY OF ILLUSTRATING THE CHARACTERS OF BOTH MOTHER AND SON.

III.

Playing Soldier

WHEREIN THE YOUNG READER WILL FIND HOW GEORGE FIGURED AS A LITTLE SOLDIER AT SCHOOL; WITH SOME REMARKS TOUCHING HIS WONDERFUL STRENGTH AND ACTIVITY OF BODY, AND COURAGE OF SPIRIT; AND HOW HE WOULD HAVE FIGURED AS A LITTLE SAILOR, HAD HE NOT BEEN PREVENTED BY A MOTHER'S ANXIOUS LOVE; WHICH INFLUENCED NOT ONLY THE WHOLE COURSE OF HIS FUTURE LIFE, BUT ALSO THE DESTINY OF HIS NATIVE COUNTRY, AND, IT MAY BE, THAT OF THE WHOLE WORLD; AS THE LITTLE READER WILL FIND OUT FOR HIMSELF. IF HE BUT HAVE THE PATIENCE TO BEAR UNCLE JUVINELL COMPANY TO THE END OF THIS INTERESTING HISTORY.

IV.

"Rules of Behavior"

AFFORDING TO THE READER ANOTHER AND HIS LAST GLIMPSE OF WASHINGTON AS A SCHOOL-BOY. HERE HE WILL LEARN OF WASHINGTON'S MANY INGENIOUS MODES OF GAINING AND RETAINING KNOWLEDGE, AND HIS HABITS OF PUTTING IT TO PRACTICAL USES; AND WILL FIND HIS RULES OF BEHAVIOR IN COMPANY AND IN CONVERSATION, WRITTEN AT THE AGE OF THIRTEEN, WHICH UNCLE JUVINELL WOULD EARNESTLY RECOMMEND HIM, AND, IN FACT, ALL HIS READERS, BE THEY BOYS OR GIRLS, MEN OR WOMEN, TO STORE AWAY IN THEIR MEMORIES, IF THEY BE DESIROUS OF GROWING IN VIRTUE. AND OF DEPORTING THEMSELVES IN SUCH A MANNER AS TO GAIN THE GOOD-WILL AND ESTEEM, AND CONTRIBUTE TO THE HAPPINESS, OF ALL AROUND THEM.

V.

In the Wilderness

IN WHICH WILL BE SEEN HOW GEORGE BECAME ACQUAINTED WITH OLD LORD FAIRFAX, AND WAS EMPLOYED BY THIS GREAT NOBLEMAN TO ACT AS SURVEYOR OF ALL HIS WILD LANDS; WITH SOME ACCOUNT OF THE LIFE HE LED IN THE WILDERNESS, AND A SOMEWHAT HIGHLY COLORED PICTURE OF A WAR-DANCE PERFORMED BY A PARTY OF INDIANS FOR THE ENTERTAINMENT OF HIM AND HIS FRIENDS.

VI.

The Young Surveyor

REVEALING STILL FURTHER GLIMPSES OF WASHINGTON AS A YOUNG SURVEYOR,—IN WHICH THE READER WILL SEE HOW THAT GREAT MAN BROUGHT HIS LABORS IN THE WILDERNESS TO AN END; WITH SOME REMARKS RESPECTING THE LOWLAND BEAUTY, AND HOW LITTLE IS KNOWN OF HER.

VII.

First Military Appointment

IN WHICH THE YOUNG READER WILL LEARN HOW WASHINGTON, AT THE EARLY AGE OF NINETEEN, BECAME ONE OF THE ADJUTANT-GENERALS OF THE PROVINCE OF VIRGINIA; AND HOW HE WENT ON A VOYAGE TO THE WEST INDIES IN COMPANY WITH HIS BROTHER LAWRENCE, WHO, BEING IN QUEST OF HEALTH, AND FAILING TO FIND IT THERE, RETURNED HOME TO DIE.

VIII.

Important Explanations

WHEREIN UNCLE JUVINELL AND THE LITTLE FOLKS TALK TOGETHER, IN A PLEASING AND FAMILIAR STYLE OF CERTAIN MATTERS CONTAINED IN THE FOREGOING PAGES; WHICH, BEING SOMEWHAT DIFFICULT OF COMPREHENSION, NEED TO BE MORE FULLY AND CLEARLY EXPLAINED, THAT THEY MAY THE BETTER UNDERSTAND WHAT IS TO COME HEREAFTER IN THIS INTERESTING HISTORY.

IX.

Indian Troubles

WHEREIN UNCLE JUVINELL GOES ON WITH HIS STORY, AND TELLS THE LITTLE FOLKS ALL THAT IS NEEDFUL FOR THEM TO KNOW CONCERNING THE CAUSES THAT BROUGHT ABOUT THE OLD FRENCH WAR; TO WHICH THE YOUNG READER WILL DO WELL TO PAY VERY PARTICULAR ATTENTION.

X.

"Big Talk" with "White Thunder"

EXPLAINING HOW MAJOR WASHINGTON CAME TO BE SENT BY GOVERNOR DINWIDDIE ON A MISSION TO THE FRENCH, NEAR LAKE ERIE.—HOW HE SET OUT.—WHAT BEFELL HIM BY THE WAY.—HOW HE STOPPED AT LOGSTOWN TO HAVE A BIG TALK WITH THE HALF-KING, WHITE THUNDER, AND OTHER INDIAN WORTHIES.—HOW HE AT LAST REACHED THE FRENCH FORT, AND WHAT HE DID AFTER HE GOT THERE.

XI.

Christmas in the Wilderness

ENABLING THE YOUNG READER TO FOLLOW MAJOR WASHINGTON TO HIS JOURNEY'S END, AND SEE HOW HE AND HIS PARTY SPENT THEIR CHRISTMAS IN THE WILDERNESS.—HOW HE TWICE CAME NEAR LOSING HIS LIFE, FIRST BY THE TREACHERY OF AN INDIAN GUIDE, AND THEN BY DROWNING; WITH SOME ACCOUNT OF HIS INTERVIEW WITH THE INDIAN PRINCESS, ALIQUIPPA.

XII.

Washington's First Battle

IN WHICH THE YOUNG READER, AFTER GETTING A HINT OF THE TREMENDOUS CONSEQUENCES THAT ENSUED FROM THE FRENCH GENERAL'S LETTER, WILL FIND SO MUCH TO ENTERTAIN HIM, THAT HE WILL READILY EXCUSE UNCLE JUVINELL FROM GIVING THE REMAINING HEADS OF THIS CHAPTER; FURTHER THAN TO SAY, THAT IT WINDS UP WITH QUITE A LIVELY AND SPIRITED ACCOUNT OF WASHINGTON'S FIRST BATTLE.

XIII.

Fort Necessity

WHAT BEFELL COLONEL WASHINGTON IN AND AROUND FORT NECESSITY, AND HOW HE SUSTAINED HIS FIRST SIEGE; WHICH WILL BE FOUND EVEN MORE ENTERTAINING THAN THE ACCOUNT OF HIS FIRST BATTLE, NARRATED IN THE LAST CHAPTER.

XIV.

General Braddock

IN WHICH THE YOUNG READER AND COLONEL WASHINGTON FORM THE ACQUAINTANCE OF GENERAL BRADDOCK, AND COME TO THE SAME CONCLUSIONS REGARDING HIS CHARACTER; AND IN WHICH THE READER IS HONORED WITH A SLIGHT INTRODUCTION TO THE GREAT DR. FRANKLIN, WHO GIVES SOME GOOD ADVICE, WHICH BRADDOCK, TO HIS FINAL COST, FAILS TO FOLLOW; AND IS ENTERTAINED WITH A FEW GLIMPSES OF LIFE IN CAMP.

XV.

Rough Work

THE READER WILL SEE HOW GENERAL BRADDOCK AT LAST SET OUT ON HIS MARCH TO FORT DUQUESNE.—HOW HE GOT ENTANGLED IN THE WILDERNESS, AND WAS FORCED TO CALL UPON THE YOUNG PROVINCIAL COLONEL FOR ADVICE. WHICH, THOUGH WISELY GIVEN, WAS NOT WISELY FOLLOWED.—HOW CAPTAIN JACK MADE AN OFFER, FOR WHICH HE GOT BUT SORRY THANKS; AND WILL FIND A SPRINKLING OF WAYSIDE ITEMS HERE AND THERE; WHICH SAVES THIS CHAPTER FROM BEING CONSIDERED A DULL ONE.

XVI.

Braddock's Defeat

IN WHICH IS RECORDED THE BLOODIEST PAGE IN THE ANNALS OF AMERICA; OR, TO EXPRESS IT OTHERWISE, AN ACCOUNT OF THE FAMOUS BATTLE OF THE MONONGAHELA, COMMONLY CALLED BRADDOCK'S DEFEAT; WHICH, IT WILL BE SEEN AT A GLANCE, MIGHT HAVE TURNED OUT A VICTORY AS WELL, HAD WASHINGTON'S ADVICE BEEN FOLLOWED.

XVII.

Explanations

WHEREIN UNCLE JUVINELL AND THE LITTLE FOLKS DISCOURSE TOGETHER, IN A LIVELY AND ENTERTAINING STYLE, OF DIVERS MATTERS TO BE FOUND, AND NOT TO BE FOUND, IN BOOK THURSDAY; WHICH MAY SEEM OF LITTLE CONSEQUENCE TO THOSE ELDERLY PEOPLE WHO ARE TOO WISE TO BE AMUSED, AND WHO WOULD, ANY TIME, RATHER SEE A FACT BROUGHT OUT STARK NAKED THAN DRESSED HANDSOMELY. SUCH OWLS ARE REQUESTED TO PASS OVER THIS CHAPTER, AND PERCH UPON BOOK FRIDAY, PORTIONS OF WHICH WILL, BE FOUND QUITE AS DRY AS THEY COULD POSSIBLY DESIRE.

XVIII.

Work in Earnest

SHOWING HOW BRADDOCK'S ARMY CONTINUED ITS FLIGHT TO PHILADELPHIA.—HOW WASHINGTON RETURNED TO MOUNT VERNON, AND WAS SHORTLY AFTERWARDS MADE COMMANDER OF ALL THE FORCES OF VIRGINIA; AND HOW HE WENT TO BOSTON, AND WHY; WITH OTHER ITEMS OF INTEREST.

XIX.

Dark Days

STILL FARTHER ACCOUNT OF WASHINGTON'S TROUBLES WITH THE INDIANS AND WITH HIS OWN MEN, AND NOTICE OF HIS MISUNDERSTANDING WITH GOVERNOR DINWIDDIE; ALL OF WHICH, COMBINED, RENDER THIS THE SADDEST AND THE GLOOMIEST PERIOD OF HIS LIFE.

XX.

A New Enterprise

CONTAINING GLIMPSES OUTSIDE OF THE DIRECT LINE OF OUR STORY, WITH A MORE MINUTE AND CIRCUMSTANTIAL ACCOUNT OF HOW WASHINGTON WOOED AND WON A FAIR LADY THAN IS TO BE MET WITH ELSEWHERE; WITH SOME PARTICULARS TOUCHING AN INTENDED EXPEDITION AGAINST FORT DUQUESNE.

XXI.

More Blundering

SHOWING HOW BRADDOCK'S FOLLY WAS REPEATED BY MAJOR GRANT, AS FOREBODED BY WASHINGTON; AND ALSO WHAT CAME OF THE EXPEDITION AGAINST FORT DUQUESNE.

XXII.

Washington at Home

GIVING AN ACCOUNT OF WASHINGTON'S MARRIAGE WITH MRS. CUSTIS.—HIS RECEPTION BY THE VIRGINIA HOUSE OF BURGESSES.—HIS HABITS AS A MAN OF BUSINESS.—HIS RURAL PURSUITS AND AMUSEMENTS.—HIS LOVE OF SOCIAL PLEASURES.—HIS ADVENTURE WITH A POACHER; AND MANY OTHER ITEMS; ALL OF WHICH, COMBINED, MAKE THIS CHAPTER ONE OF THE MOST PLEASING AND ENTERTAINING OF THE WHOLE BOOK.

XXIII.

A Family Quarrel

WHEREIN THE YOUNG READER WILL FIND WHAT WILL BE EXPLAINED MORE TO HIS SATISFACTION IN CHAPTER XXIV.

XXIV.

The Cause of the Quarrel

AFFORDING A MORE CLEAR, AND SATISFACTORY ACCOUNT OF THE CAUSES THAT BROUGHT ABOUT OUR REVOLUTIONARY WAR THAN WAS GIVEN IN CHAPTER XXIII; BUT CHAPTER XXV. MUST NEEDS BE READ, BEFORE A FULL AND COMPLETE UNDERSTANDING OF THESE MATTERS CAN BE ARRIVED AT.

XXV.

Resistance to Tyranny

ILLUSTRATING WHAT PART WASHINGTON TOOK IN THESE MEASURES OF RESISTANCE TO BRITISH TYRANNY.—HOW HE BECAME A REPRESENTATIVE OF VIRGINIA IN THE GREAT COLONIAL ASSEMBLY, OTHERWISE CALLED THE OLD CONTINENTAL CONGRESS; AND HOW, UPON THE BREAKING-OUT OF HOSTILITIES BETWEEN THE COLONIES AND THE MOTHER-COUNTRY, HE WAS MADE COMMANDER-IN-CHIEF OF ALL THE FORCES OF THE UNITED COLONIES; WITH OTHER ITEMS TOUCHING THE PROCEEDINGS OF THE CONTINENTAL CONGRESS, AND PATRICK HENRY, THE GREAT VIRGINIA ORATOR.

XXVI.

Conclusion

WHEREIN THE YOUNG READER WILL BE ENTERTAINED WITH THE PLEASING AND EDIFYING CONVERSATION WHICH TOOK PLACE BETWEEN UNCLE JUVINELL AND THE LITTLE FOLKS, TOUCHING DIVERS MATTERS IN BOOK FRIDAY; WHICH DEMAND FURTHER CONSIDERATION FOR A MORE COMPLETE UNDERSTANDING OF OUR HISTORY, PAST AND TO COME.

INTRODUCTION.

Somewhere in green Kentucky, not a great many years ago, the ruddy light of a Christmas sunset, streaming in at the windows of an old-fashioned brick house, that stood on a gentle hillside, half hidden by evergreens, shone full and broad on a group of merry little youngsters there met together to spend the holiday with their Uncle Juvinell, a charming old bachelor of threescore and ten.

What with "blind man's buff," "leap-frog," "hide-and-seek," "poor pussy wants a corner," Mother Goose, dominos, sky-rockets and squibs, and what with the roasting of big red apples and the munching of gingerbread elephants, the reading of beautiful story-books,—received that morning as Christmas presents from their Uncle Juvinell and other loving relatives,—these little folks had found this day the most delightful of their lives.

Tired at last of play, and stuffed with Christmas knick-knacks till their jackets and breeches could hold no more, they had now betaken themselves to the library to await the return of their Uncle Juvinell, who had gone out to take his usual evening walk; and were now quietly seated round a blazing winter fire, that winked and blinked at them with its great bright eye, and went roaring right merrily up the wide chimney. Just as the last beam of the setting sun went out at the window, Uncle Juvinell, as if to fill its place, came in at the door, all brisk and ruddy from his tramp over the snow in the sharp bracing air, and was hailed with a joyous shout by the little folks, who, hastening to wheel his great arm-chair for him round to the fire, pushed and pulled him into it, and called upon him to tell one of his most charming stories, even before the tingling frost was out of his nose.

As this worthy old gentleman has done much for the entertainment and instruction of the rising generations of the land, it is but due him that some mention, touching his many amiable traits of character and his accomplishments of mind and person, should be made in this place for the more complete satisfaction of those who may hereafter feel themselves indebted to him for some of the most pleasant moments of their lives.

In person, Uncle Juvinell is stout and well-rounded. His legs are fat, and rather short; his body is fat, and rather long; his belly is snug and plump; his hands are plump and white; his hair is white and soft; his eyes are soft and blue; his coat is blue and sleek; and over his sleek and dimpled face, from his dimpled chin to the very crown of his head,—which, being bald, shines like sweet oil in a warm fire-light,—there beams one unbroken smile of fun, good-humor, and love, that fills one's heart with sunshine to behold. Indeed, to look at him, and be with him a while, you could hardly help half believing that he must be a twin-brother of Santa Claus, so closely does he resemble that far-famed personage, not only in appearance, but in character also; and more than once, having been met in his little sleigh by some belated school-boy, whistling homeward through the twilight of a Christmas or New Year's Eve, he has been mistaken for the jolly old saint himself. In short, his whole appearance is in the highest degree respectable; and there is even about him an air of old-fashioned elegance, which of course is owing chiefly to the natural sweetness and politeness of his manners, and yet perhaps a little heightened withal by the gold-bowed spectacles that he wears on his nose, the heavy gold bar that pins his snowy linen, the gold buttons that shine on his coat, his massive gold watch-chain (at the end of which hangs a great red seal as big as a baby's fist), and by his gold-headed ebony cane, that he always carries on his shoulder like a musket when he walks, as much as to say, "Threescore and ten, and no need of a staff yet, my Christian friend." No man is more beloved and esteemed by all who know him, old and young, than he; for like Father Grimes, whose nephew he is by the mother's side.—

> "He modest merit seeks to find,
>   And give it its desert;
> He has no malice in his mind,
>   No ruffles on his shirt.
>
> His neighbors he does not abuse;
>   Is sociable and gay:
> He wears large buckles in his shoes,
>   And changes them, each day."

If there is one thing about Uncle Juvinell that we might venture to pronounce more charming than another, it is the smile of mingled fun, good-humor, and love, with which his countenance never ceases to shine, save when he hears the voice of pain and his breast with pity burns. Touching this same trait of his, a lady once said in our hearing, that she verily believed a cherub, fresh from the rosy chambers of the morning, came at the opening of each day to Uncle Juvinell's chamber, just on purpose to dash a handful of sunbeams on his head; and, as there were always more than enough to keep his face bathed with smiles for the next twenty-four hours, they were not wasted, but, falling and lodging on his gold spectacles, his gold breast-pin, his gold buttons, his gold watch-chain, and the gold head of his ebony cane, washed them with lustre ever new, as if his face, bright and broad as it was, were not enough to reflect the love and sunshine ever dwelling in his heart. We will not undertake to vouch for the truth of this, however. As the young lady was a marriageable young lady, and had been for a number of years, it would not be gallant or generous for us to mention it; but of this we are certain, that, when this good old gentleman enters a room, there is a warmth and brightness in his very presence, that causes you to look round, half expecting to see the tables and chairs throwing their shadows along the floor, as if, by the power of magic, a window had suddenly been opened in the wall to let in the morning sunshine.

If the affections of Uncle Juvinell's heart are childlike in their freshness, the powers of his intellect are gigantic in their dimensions. He is a man of prodigious learning: for proof of which, you have but to enter his library, and take note of the books upon books that crowd the shelves from the floor to the ceiling; the maps that line the walls; the two great globes, one of the earth and the other of the heavens, that stand on either side of his reading-desk; and the reading-desk itself, whereon there always lies some book of monstrous size, wide open, which no one has ever had the courage to read from beginning to end, or could comprehend if he did.

In the languages he is very expert; speaking French with such clearness and distinctness, that any native-born Frenchman, with a fair knowledge of the English, can with but little difficulty understand more than half he says; and in German he is scarcely less fluent and ready; while his Latin is the envy of all who know only their mother-tongue. In mathematics, his skill is such, that you might give him a sum, the working-out of which would cover three or four large slates; and he would never fail to arrive at the answer, let him but take his time.

In astronomy, he is perfectly at home among the fixed stars; can distinguish them at a single glance, and that, too, without the help of his spectacles, from the wandering planets; and is as familiar with the motion and changes of the moon, as if he had been in the habit for the last forty years of spending the hot summer months at some of the fashionable watering-places of that amiable and interesting orb. But it is in the history of the nations and great men of the earth that Uncle Juvinell most excels, as shall be proved to your entire satisfaction before reaching the end of this volume.

And yet, notwithstanding the vastness of his learning and the gigantic powers of his mind, he can, when it so pleases him, disburden himself of these great matters, and descend from his lofty height to the comprehension of the little folks, with as much ease as a huge balloon, soaring amidst the clouds, can let off its gas, and sink down to the level of the kites, air-balls, and sky-rockets wherewith they are wont to amuse themselves.

Being an old bachelor, as before noticed, he, of course, has no children of his own; but, like the philosopher that he is, he always consoles himself for this misfortune with the reflection, that, had he been so favored, much of his love and affection must needs have been wasted on his own six, eight, or ten, as the case might have been, instead of being divided without measure among the hundreds and thousands of little ones that gladden the wedded life, and fill with their music the homes of others more blessed.

Living, as all his brothers do, in easy circumstances, he has abundant time and leisure to devote himself to the particular interest and enjoyment of these little ones; and is always casting in his mind what he may be doing to amuse them, or make them wiser, better, and happier.

Such is the ease, heartiness, and familiarity with which he demeans himself when among them, and enters into all their little pastimes and concerns, that they stand no more in awe of him than if he were one of their own number; and make him the butt of a thousand impish pranks, at which he laughs as heartily as the merriest rogue among them. And yet it is for that very reason, perhaps, that they love him so devotedly, and would give up their dog-knives or wax dolls any day, sooner than show themselves unmindful of his slightest wishes, or do aught that could bring upon them even his softest rebuke. They make nothing of taking off his gold spectacles, and putting them on their own little pugs to look wise; or running their chubby fists into the tight, warm pockets of his breeches, in quest of his gold pencil or pearl-handled knife; or dashing like mad over the yard, with his gold-headed cane for a steed; or stealing up behind him, as he stands with his back to the fire, and slyly pulling out his big red bandanna handkerchief, wherewith to yoke the dog and cat together as they lie sociably side by side on the hearth-rug. In short, he will suffer them to tease him and tousle him and tumble him to their hearts' content, and set no limits to their liberties, so long as they are careful not to touch his snowy linen with their smutched fingers; for, if Uncle Juvinell has one fault in the world, it is his unreasonable partiality for snowy linen. But, were we to go on with our praises and commendations of this best of men, we should fill a large volume full to overflowing, and still leave the better half unsaid: so we must exercise a little self-denial, and forego such pleasing thoughts for the present, as it now behooves us to bring our minds to bear upon matters we have more nearly in view.

Seeing how earnestly the little folks were bent upon drawing out of him one of his longest stories, Uncle Juvinell now bade them sit down and be quiet till he should have time to conjure up something more charming than any Arabian tale they had ever heard; and throwing himself back in his great arm-chair, and fixing his eyes on the glowing coals, that seemed to present to his fancy an ever-shifting panorama, was soon lost in profound meditation. And the longer he thought, the harder he looked at the fire, which knowingly answered his look with a winking and blinking of its great bright eye, that seemed to say, "Well, Uncle Juvinell, what shall we do for the entertainment or instruction of these little people to-night? Shall we tell them of that crew of antic goblins we wot of, who are wont to meet by moonlight, to play at football with the hanged man's head, among the tombstones of an old graveyard? Or may be that dreadful ogre, with the one fiery eye in the middle of his forehead, who was in the habit of roasting fat men on a spit for his Christmas dinners, would be more to their taste. Or, if you prefer it, let it be that beautiful fairy, who, mounted on a milk-white pony, and dressed in green and gold, made her home in an echoing wood, for no other purpose than to lead little children therefrom, who might by some ill chance be separated from their friends, and lose their way in its tangled wilds. Or perhaps you are thinking it would be more instructive to them were we to conjure up some story of early times in green Kentucky, when our great-grandfathers were wont to take their rifles to bed with them, and sleep with them in their arms, ready to spring up at the slightest rustling of the dry leaves in the woods, and defend themselves against the dreaded Indian, as with panther-like tread he skulked around their lonely dwellings."

To each and all of these, Uncle Juvinell shook his head; none of them being just exactly the thing he wanted. At length, finding that the fire hindered rather than helped him to make a choice, he rose from his seat, turned his back upon it, and looked from one bright face to another of the circle before him, till his eye rested on Daniel, who was among the oldest of the children, and was, by the way, the young historian of the family, and, in his own opinion, a youth of rather uncommon parts. He had that morning received from his uncle, as a Christmas present, that most delightful of story-books, "Robinson Crusoe;" but having seen the unlucky sailor high, but not dry, on his desert island, and having run his eye over all the pictures, he had laid it aside, and was now standing at the reading-desk, looking as wise as a young owl in a fog over a very large book indeed, in which he pretended to be too deeply interested to finish a slab of gingerbread that lay half munched at his side.

Seeing his little nephew thus engaged, Uncle Juvinell smiled a quiet smile all to himself, and, after watching him a few moments, said, "Dannie, my boy, what book is that you are reading with so much interest that you have forgotten your gingerbread?"

"Irving's Life of Washington, sir," replied Daniel with an air.

"A good book, a very good indeed; but too hard for you, I fear," said Uncle Juvinell, shaking his head. "Tell me, though, how far you have read."

"To Braddock's defeat, sir," replied Daniel.

"You have been getting over the ground rather fast, I am thinking; but tell me how you like it," said Uncle Juvinell, by way of drawing his little nephew out.

"Here and there, I come to a chapter that I like very much," replied Daniel: "but there are parts that I don't understand very well; and I was just thinking that I would point them out to you some time, and get you to explain them to me; as you will, I am certain; for you know every thing, and are so obliging to us little folks!"

At this, Uncle Juvinell's face lighted up as with a brilliant thought; but, without seeming to notice his little nephew's request just then, he reseated himself, and again began looking hard at the fire. The fire opened its great bright eye more widely than before, and looked as if it were putting the question, "Well, sir, and what is it now? Out with it, and I will throw what light I can on the matter." After a few moments, there appeared to be a perfect understanding between them; for the fire with a sly wink seemed to say, "A happy thought, Uncle Juvinell,—a very happy thought indeed: I was just on the point of proposing the very same thing myself. Come, let us go about it at once, and make these holidays the brightest and happiest these little folks have ever known, or ever could or would or should know, in all their lives." And the fire fell to winking and blinking at such an extravagant rate, that the shadows of those who were seated round it began bobbing up and down the wall, looking like misshapen goblins amusing themselves by jumping imaginary ropes, the gigantic one of Uncle Juvinell leaping so high as to butt the ceiling.

After several minutes of deep thought, the old gentleman rose, and stood on his short fat legs with the air of a man who had made up his mind, and with a smile on his face, as if sure he was just on the point of giving them all a pleasant surprise. "Laura, my dear," said he, "take down that picture from the wall you see hanging to the right of the bookcase; and you, Ella, my darling, take that bunch of feathers, and brush off the dust from it. Now hand it to me. This, my cherubs," he went on, "is the portrait of the good and great George Washington, who is called the Father of our country. It is to him, more than to any other man, that we owe the blessings of freedom, peace, and prosperity, we now enjoy in larger measure than any other people of the wide earth; and it was for these same blessings that he fought and struggled through all the weary years of our Revolutionary War, amidst difficulties, dangers, and discouragements such as never before tried the strength of man. And when, in the happy end, he, by his courage, skill, and fortitude, and abiding trust in the protection of an all-wise Providence, had come out victorious over all, and driven our cruel enemies from the land, so that our homes were once more gladdened with the smiles of peace and plenty,—then it was that a grateful people with one voice hailed him chosen of the Lord for the salvation of our beloved country. Blessed be the name of George Washington,—blessed for evermore!" And a big tear of love and thankfulness started from each of Uncle Juvinell's mild blue eyes, trickled slowly over his ruddy cheek, and, dropping thence, went hopping and sparkling down his large blue waistcoat.

At this the little folks looked very grave, and thought to themselves, "What a good man Washington must have been, and how much he must have done and suffered for the welfare of his fellow-beings, thus to have brought the tears to our dear old uncle's eyes!" After looking at the picture for some moments in silence, they began talking about it, each in his or her own fashion; while Uncle Juvinell listened with much interest, curious to see what different impressions it would produce on their minds.

"That scroll he holds in his left hand must be his farewell address to his army," said Daniel, the young historian, looking very wise.

"What a fine long sword he carries at his side!" said Bryce, a war-like youngster who had just climbed to the summit of his ninth year, and had, as you must know, a wooden sword of his own, with which he went about dealing death and destruction to whole regiments of cornstalks and squadrons of horse-weeds, calling them British and Tories.

"How tall and grand and handsome he looks!" said Laura, a prim and demure little miss of thirteen: "in his presence, I am sure I could never speak above a whisper."

"That, yonder, among the trees and evergreens on the hill, must be the house where he lived," said Ella, a modest, sweet-mannered little lady of twelve. "What a beautiful place it is! and what a happy home it must have been when he lived in it!"

"And see how the hill slopes down to the river, so grassy and smooth! and such a nice place for little boys to roll over and over down to the bottom!" said Ned, a rough-and-tumble youngster of ten, who spent one-half of the sunshine with his back to the ground and his heels in the air.

"And see the beautiful river so broad and so smooth, and the great ships afar off going down to the sea!" said Johnnie, a little poet of eight, who passed much of his time dreaming with his eyes open.

"And such a pretty play-house as I see there among the bushes on the hillside!" said Fannie, a stout little matron of five, the mother of a large and still increasing family of dolls.

"That is not a play-house, Fannie, but the tomb where Washington lies buried," said Dannie with an air of superior wisdom.

"What a splendid white horse that black man is holding for him! How he bows his neck, and champs his bit, and paws the ground!" said Willie, a harum-scarum, neck-or-nothing young blade of fourteen, who would have given his best leg to have been the owner of a galloping, high-headed, short-tailed pony.

"What is he doing so far away from home without his hat, I wonder?" said Master Charlie, a knowing young gentleman of eight, who was much in the habit of doubting everybody's eyes and ears but his own.

"How kind and good he looks out of his eyes, just like father!" said Mary, an affectionate and timid little creature of seven.

Just then, Addison, a plump little fellow of four, in all the glory of his first new jacket and his first new breeches, who was standing on the top round of Uncle Juvinell's chair, suddenly cried out in a very strong voice for his age, "Oh! he looks just like Uncle Juvinell: now don't he, Cousin Mary?"

For a man of his appearance to be thus compared with so stately and dignified a man as Washington was a thing so ludicrous, that Uncle Juvinell was surprised into the heartiest fit of laughter that he had enjoyed that day. When it was over, he bade Laura hang up the picture again in its accustomed place, and began where he had left off some time before: "Now, my dear children, it came into my mind, while I was talking with your Cousin Dannie a little bit ago, that I could not tell you any thing more entertaining and instructive than the story of Washington's life. It will, I am quite sure, interest you much: for although he was such a great man,—the greatest, no doubt, that ever lived,—and so awful to look upon, yet, for all that, his heart was full to overflowing with the most tender and kindly affections, and, if you can believe it, quite as fond of little children as your Uncle Juvinell; often joining in their innocent sports for a whole hour at a time. Let me see. This is Wednesday; and we have seven, eight, long holidays before us to be as happy as skylarks in. Now, I am thinking, that, if we would have next New Year's Day find us better and wiser, we could not hit upon a more proper plan for beginning so desirable an end than by spending a part of each day in making ourselves acquainted with the life and character of this good and great man, and, at the close of each evening's lesson, talking over what we have learned, to our more complete understanding of the same. And now, my merry ones, speak out, and tell me what you think of it."

"It will be just exactly the very thing," said wise Daniel.

"Glorious!" said rollicking Willie.

"Charming!" said prim and demure Miss Laura.

"'Twill be delightful, I am sure," said modest Ella.

"Nothing could please me better, if we have a good big battle now and then," said war-like Bryce.

"I wonder if it will be as interesting as 'Robinson Crusoe'?" put in doubting Charlie.

"Or 'Aladdin and his Wonderful Lamp'?" chimed in dreaming Johnnie.

"And we'll all listen, and be so good!" said timid, loving little Mary.

"Wait a moment for me, uncle, till I run down to the cabin, just to see how Black Daddy's getting along making my sled," said hair-brained Ned.

"And wait a little bit for me too, uncle, till I go and put my dolly babe to bed; for she might take the measles if I keep her up too long," said motherly Fannie.

"And let me sit on your knee, uncle; Cousin Mary wants my chair," said Addison, the youngest one of them all, at the same time climbing up, and getting astride of Uncle Juvinell's left fat leg.

"Then settle yourselves at once, you noisy chatterboxes," said Uncle Juvinell with a shining face; "and mind you be as quiet and mute as mice at a cat's wedding while I am telling my story, or I'll"—His threat was drowned in the joyous shouts of the children as they scrambled into their chairs. When they had all put on a listening look, he poured out a little yellow, squat, Dutch mug brimful of rich brown cider from a big blue pitcher that Black Daddy had just placed on a table close at hand, and, having wet his whistle therewith, began his story. And now and then, as the story went on, the fire, keeping its bright, watchful eye upon the old gentleman, would wink at him in a sly manner, that seemed to say, "Well done, Uncle Juvinell,—very well done indeed. You see, sir, I was quite right in what I told you. We have hit upon the very thing. The little folks are enchanted: they are drawing in wisdom with every breath. A merry Christmas to us all!" Pop, pop! hurrah! pop!

The Farmer Boy and How He Became Commander-in-Chief

I.

GEORGE AT SCHOOL.

A hundred years ago or more, there stood on the green slopes of the Potomac, in the county of Westmoreland, Va., an old red farmhouse, with a huge stone chimney at each end, and high gray roof, the eaves of which projected in such a manner as to cover a porch in front and two or three small shed-rooms in the rear. Now, although this house was built of wooden beams and painted boards, and was far from being what could be called, even for those times, a fine one,—looking as it did more like a barn than a dwelling for man,—yet, for all that, it had the honor of being the birthplace of the good and great George Washington, who is said, by many very wise persons who ought to know, to have been the greatest man that ever came into this pleasant and glorious world of ours.

His father, Augustine Washington, was married early in life to Jane Butler, who died after having borne him two sons, Lawrence and Augustine. In a year or two after this loss, feeling the want of some one to gladden his lonely heart and home, he married Mary Ball, the belle of Horseneck, and said to have been the most beautiful young lady in all that part of the country. By this union he was blessed with six children, of whom our George, the eldest, was born on the twenty-second day of February, in the year of our Lord one thousand seven hundred and thirty-two.

It has often appeared strange to me that nothing should be known of this great man's life up to the completion of his fifth year: and I am sorry for your sakes, my little ones, that such is the case; for it would be such a nice beginning to our story, could we say with certainty that he distinguished himself by walking alone at the age of five months; that he could pronounce "Mother" and "Good" with perfect distinctness when but one year old; that his mother taught him at the age of two to kneel by her side, and lisp, before going to his evening rest, that beautiful prayer, beginning with, "Now I lay me down to sleep;" that he rode like mad, at the age of three, round and round the yard, on his father's buckhorn-headed cane; and that he rode on

The Farmer Boy and How He Became Commander-in-Chief

a real horse at the age of four, and went galloping like a young Tartar round and round the meadow in front of the house, to the delight of his young mother, who watched him from the window. Of all this, and a great deal more of the same sort, you would, I doubt not, like much to hear, and I would like much to tell you; but we must keep within the bounds of true history, and content ourselves with the knowledge of that which really did happen. With this safe rule for our guidance, we will therefore proceed at once to take up the thread of our story at that period of George's boyhood, concerning which some certain record has come down to our time.

At the age of five, when he was old enough to walk all alone for a mile or two through the woods and fields, his parents started him to school one bright spring morning, with his little basket on his arm, containing his dinner and a bran-new spelling-book, to take his first tiny steps in the flowery path of knowledge.

His first teacher was a Mr. Hobby, an old man, who lived on a distant part of his father's plantation, and is said to have been besides the sexton or grave-digger of the neighborhood; and was, I have my private reasons for thinking, a broken-down old soldier, with a big cocked hat that shaded a kindly and weather-beaten face, and a wooden leg,—an ornament for which he was indebted to a cannon-ball, and took more pride in than if it had been a sound one of flesh and bone. As it is rarely ever the case that men with wooden legs are called upon to fight the battles of their country, this worthy old man, who well knew how to read and write, and cipher too, must needs earn his livelihood by teaching school, and sowing his knowledge broadcast among the little children of the neighborhood.

Accordingly, it was to old Mr. Hobby, as everybody called him, that George was indebted for his first insight into the mysteries of book-learning; and although he was in due time to become the greatest man of this or any other age or country, yet he began his education by first learning his A B C, just as did other boys of that day, just as they are now doing, and just as they will continue to do for all time to come. After he had taken his A B C into his memory, and set them there in a straight row each in its proper place, he was not long, depend upon it, in reaching the middle of his spelling-book; and as

The Farmer Boy and How He Became Commander-in-Chief

soon as he could, without anybody's help, climb over tall and difficult words of five or six syllables, such as "immortality" or "responsibility," his master put him in the English Reader, where he soon overtook and went clean ahead of boys a great deal older than himself. From reading, he in a short time rose to writing; and it was said by those who knew him best, that he learned to write a neat round hand without ever once blotting his copy-book; and furthermore, that such a thing as a dirty, thumb-worn, dog-eared book was never seen in his hand. His next step in the path of knowledge was arithmetic; and, in less time than you can well believe, he had got the multiplication-table so thoroughly by heart, that he could run over it as fast backwards, from twelve times twelve to twice one, as common boys straightforward, even with the open book before their eyes. So well did he study, that, in less than four years' time after his first starting to school, the single rule of three was no more to him than long division to most boys; and he could repeat the tables of weights and measures as glibly as you, Master Johnnie, can rattle off the charming story of "Old Mother Hubbard and her Wonderful Dog."

Now, the rapid progress George made in his studies was owing not so much to his uncommon aptitude at learning as to the diligence and industry with which he applied himself to them. For example: when other boys would be staring out at the window, watching the birds and squirrels sporting among the tree-tops; or sitting idly with their hands in their pockets, opening and shutting their jack-knives, or counting their marbles, or munching apples and corn-dodgers in a sneaking and unbecoming manner behind their books; or, more naughty still, shooting paper bullets at old Hobby's wooden leg as he eat dozing behind his high desk of a drowsy summer afternoon,—our George, with his hands to his ears to keep out the schoolroom buzz, would be studying with all his might; nor would he once raise his eyes from his book till every word of his lesson was ready to drop from his tongue's end of its own accord. So well did he apply himself, and so attentive was he to every thing taught him, that, by the time he was ten years old, he had learned all that the poor old grave-digger knew himself; and it was this worthy man's boast in after-years, that he had laid the foundation of Washington's future greatness. But what old Wooden Leg—for so they always called him when his back was turned—could not teach him at school, little George learned at home of his father and mother, who were well educated for those days; and many a long winter evening did these good parents spend in telling their children interesting and instructive stories of olden times, far-off countries, and strange people, which George would write down in his copy-book in his neatest, roundest hand, and remember ever afterward.

A more prudent and careful father, and a more discreet and affectionate mother, than Mr. Washington and his wife Mary, perhaps never lived. So earnest and watchful were they to bring up their children in the fear of the Lord, and in the practice of every noble virtue, that their dutiful behavior and sweet manners were the talk and praise of the good people for miles and miles around. They taught them to be neat and orderly in their dress, as well as civil and polite in their manners; to be respectful to their elders; to be kind to one another, and to every thing God hath made, both great and small, whether man or bird or beast: but chiefly were they concerned to teach them the love of truth, and to tell it at all times when it should be their duty to speak out, let the consequences be what they might. To show you that such wise and careful training was not lost on the tender mind of George, I will tell you the story of his little hatchet, as it may serve you good stead in the day when you may be tempted to wander astray from the path of truth and virtue.

One Christmas Eve, when the sharp, frosty air made the blood brisk and lively in the veins, little George, who was then about six years old, hung up his stocking on the mantel of the huge chimney, saying to himself as he did so, "Good Santa Claus, be kind to me while I am sleeping peacefully." Next morning, bright and early, just as a great Christmas log had begun to blaze and crackle on the hearth, he jumped spryly from his bed, and, without stopping to put on his clothes, ran to his stockings to see what good old Santa Claus had brought him while he slept. I leave you to picture to your minds his delight upon finding therein a little Indian tomahawk, with a bright keen edge and long red handle. It would have done all your hearts good to have seen how he skipped and danced around the room, and flourished his hatchet high over his head; how he went showing it to every one about the house, white and black; praising good old

The Farmer Boy and How He Became Commander-in-Chief

Santa Claus to the very skies, and never once feeling the want of his breeches. But, between you and me, I am rather inclined to suspect, that, if we had any means of arriving at the facts of the case, it would be found that Santa Claus had no more concern in this matter than your Uncle Juvinell himself. To my mind, there is more reason in the supposition, that his father, seeing the jolly old saint pass by at a late hour of the night in an empty sleigh, and that the children were not likely to have their stockings filled for that once, got up early in the morning, and put the hatchet in there himself, rather than that his little son should be disappointed.

Be this as it may, it was all the same to George; and he was as happy as happy could be. At the breakfast-table, he could hardly eat his bread and milk for looking at his shining axe, which he had laid beside him on the table; and, before it was fairly broad daylight, he was out at the wood-yard, ankle-deep in snow, cutting and chopping away at the hard-seasoned beech and maple logs, as if it lay with him, for that day at least, to keep the whole family, white and black, from freezing. By and by, however, he found this more work than play, and began to cast his earnest young eyes about him for something green and soft whereon to try the edge and temper of his hatchet. Presently, as ill-luck would have it, a fine young English cherry-tree, just over the fence hard by, caught his attention, which, without further ado, he fell to hacking might and main; and the way he made the little chips fly was a thing surprising to see.

Next morning, his father, passing by that way, saw the mischief that had been done, and was sorely displeased: for he had planted and reared this selfsame tree with the tenderest care; and, of all the trees in his orchard, there was not one other he prized so highly. Being quite sure that it was the work of some of the black children, he went straightway down to the negro quarter, bent on finding out, and bringing the unlucky culprit to a severe account.

"Dick," said he to the first one he met, "did you cut that cherry-tree?"

"No, mauster; don't know nothin' 'bout it," said Dick, showing the whites of *his* eyes.

"Did you, Sam?" said Mr. Washington, putting the same question to another little woolly-head.

"No, mauster; don't know nothin' 'bout it," said Sam, likewise showing the whites of his eyes.

The same question was put to Harry, who gave Dick and Sam's answer word for word, and, to add force to his denial, showed the whites of his eyes in like manner; and so on, till more than a dozen had been questioned with the same result; when it came to Jerry's turn to make denial, and show the whites of his eyes.

Now, you must know there was not a more audacious, mischief-making, neck-or-nothing black brat than this same Jerry to be found on the banks of the Rappahannock, which is a very long river indeed. As a fish lives in water, or a salamander in fire, so did Jerry live and breathe, and have his being, in mischief; or, in other words, mischief was the element in which Jerry found his chief delight. If any mishap befell anybody or any thing, at any hour of the day or night, on any part of the plantation, on foot or on horseback, at rest or in motion, it was sure to be brought and laid at Jerry's door. Being aware of all this, Mr. Washington was now quite sure, that, as none of the rest had cut the cherry-tree, Jerry himself must be the offender; and so he put the question to him; to which Jerry, showing the whites of his eyes, made answer, "No, mauster; I didn't cut the cherry-tree: indeed, indeed, and double deed, I didn't cut the cherry-tree."

"Ah! Jerry," said his master, "if you always told the truth, I should know when to believe you; but, as you do not, you must take the consequences of your evil ways, and blame nobody but yourself."

Upon hearing this, Jerry began dancing and hopping around the room in a very brisk and lively manner, even before his master was within ten feet of him, as if he already felt the switch about his legs.

Just then, in the very nick of time, George came walking leisurely by, hatchet in hand; who, upon seeing how matters stood, without a moment's hesitation, ran up to his father, and, dropping his hatchet, caught him round the leg, just as the first stroke of the switch was about to descend on the calves of the unlucky Jerry.

"O papa, papa!" cried he, "don't whip poor Jerry: if somebody must be whipped, let it be me; for it was I, and not Jerry, that cut the cherry-tree. I didn't know how much harm I was doing; I didn't indeed." And the child began crying piteously.

With a look of glad surprise, his father, dropping the switch, caught his brave little boy in his arms, and folded him tenderly, lovingly, to his bosom. "Now, thanks be to God," cried he, "thanks be to God, that I have a son whose love of truth is greater than his fear of punishment! Look on him, my black children, look on him, and be as near like him as you can, if you would have the love of your master and the good-will of all around you."

Seeing the unlooked-for turn the affair had taken, and not having the words to express the feelings of joy and thankfulness that swelled almost to bursting in his little black breast, Jerry darted through the door, out into the yard, kicked up his heels, yelped like a young dog, threw a somerset in the snow, and went rolling over and over down to the bottom of the hill, and ever after loved his noble little master to distraction.

The Farmer Boy and How He Became Commander-in-Chief

II.

THE FIRST SORROW.

When George had learned all that poor old Hobby could teach him, his father, to reward him for his diligence and good behavior at school, indulged him in two or three weeks' holidays, which he went to spend at a distance from home, among some friends and relatives. Here, as usual, he was made much of; for, being a great favorite with all who knew him, he met with a cordial reception wherever he went; and what with hunting and fishing, riding and visiting, the time spent here was the most delightful he had ever known. But hardly had half the happy days flown by, when word came that his father was sick, even unto death; and that, of all things, he most desired to look upon his noble boy once more before he died. With a sadness and heaviness of heart he had never before experienced, George set out on his return home, where he arrived just in time to receive his dying father's blessing. Long and deeply did he mourn his loss; for his father was most tenderly beloved by his children, and greatly esteemed by his friends and neighbors as a useful member of society, and a man of many sterling traits of character.

Mrs. Washington was thus left a young widow with a large family of young children, whom it now became her duty to provide for and educate in a manner becoming a Christian mother; and how well and faithfully and lovingly she discharged this sacred trust, is most beautifully set forth in the life and character of her great son. She was a woman of uncommon strength and clearness of understanding, and her heart was the home of every pure and noble virtue. She was mild, but firm; generous, but just; candid whenever she deemed it her duty to speak her mind, but never losing sight of the respect and consideration due to the feelings and opinions of others. She was gentle and loving with her children, yet exacting from them in return the strictest obedience to her will and wishes. But of all virtues most sacred in her eyes was that of the love of truth, which she ever sought to implant in their minds; assuring them, that, without it, all other virtues were but as unprofitable weeds, barren of fruits and flowers. She was simple and dignified in her manners, and had a hearty dislike for every thing savoring of parade and idle show. She always received her friends and visitors with a cordial smile of welcome, spreading before them with an unsparing hand the best her house afforded: but, when they rose to depart, she would invite them once, and once only, to stay longer; and, if after this they still seemed bent on going, she would do all in her power to speed them on their journey. With so many traits betokening strength of mind and character, she had but one weakness; and this was her excessive dread of thunder, caused in early maidenhood by seeing a young lady struck dead at her side by lightning.

And such was Mary, the mother of Washington; and seldom indeed has her like been seen. As her husband, by industry and prudent management, had gathered together enough of the riches of this world to leave each of his children a fine plantation, she was not hindered by straitened circumstances, or anxiety as to their means of future support, from giving her chief attention to such bodily and mental training as should have a lasting tendency to make them, in more mature years, healthy, virtuous, and wise.

It has been often remarked, that those men who have most distinguished themselves in the world's history for noble thoughts and heroic deeds, have, as a general thing, inherited those qualities of mind and heart which made them great, from their mothers, rather than from their fathers; and also that their efforts to improve and elevate the condition of their fellow-beings have been owing in a larger measure to the lessons of truth, piety, and industry, taught them by their mothers in childhood and early youth. If this be the case, then how much are we indebted for the freedom, prosperity, and happiness we now enjoy above other nations of the earth, to Mary, the mother of Washington! Perhaps, to give you a still more forcible idea of the characters of both mother and son, and of the wholesome effects on him of her judicious training, I ought to relate in this place the story of his attempt at taming the sorrel horse.

A fine horse was an object that afforded Mrs. Washington, as it did the other substantial Virginia ladies of that day, quite as much, if not more, real pleasure than their more delicate grand-daughters of the present now find in their handsome carriages, lap-dogs, and canary-birds. So great was her fondness for this noble animal, that she usually suffered two or three of her finest to run in a meadow in front of the house, where she might look at them from time to time as she sat sewing at her dining-room window. One of these was a young sorrel horse, of great beauty of form, and fleetness of foot, but of so wild and vicious a nature, that, for fear of accident, she had forbidden any one to mount him, although he had already reached his full height and size.

Now, you must know that a bolder and more skilful rider than George was not to be found in all the Old Dominion, as Virginia is sometimes called; and it was this early practice that afterwards won for him the name of being the finest horseman of his day. Often, as we may very naturally suppose to have been the case, would he reason thus with himself, as, sitting on the topmost rail of a worm fence, he watched the spirited young animal frisking and bounding about the field in all the freedom of his untamed nature: "If I were but once upon his back, with a strong bit in his mouth, believe me, I would soon make him a thing of use as well as ornament; and it would, I am sure, be such a pleasant surprise to mother to look from her window some fine morning, and see me mounted on his back, and managing him with ease, and to know that it was I who had subdued his proud spirit."

Accordingly, full of these thoughts, he arose early one bright summer morning, and invited two or three friends of his own age, then on a visit at his mother's house, to go with him to the fields, to share with him the sport, or lend their aid in carrying out his design, should it be found too difficult and hazardous for himself alone. They needed no second bidding, these young madcaps, to whom nothing could be more to their liking than such wild sport. So at it they went; and after a deal of chasing and racing, heading and doubling, falling down and picking themselves up again, and more shouting and laughing than they had breath to spare for, they at last succeeded in driving the panting and affrighted young animal into a corner. Here, by some means or other (it was difficult to tell precisely how), they managed to bridle him, although at no small risk of a broken head or two from his heels, that he seemed to fling about him

The Farmer Boy and How He Became Commander-in-Chief

in a dozen different directions at once. Having thus made him their captive, they led him out to the more open parts of the field, where George requested his friends to hold him till he could get on his back. But the wild and unruly spirit the young beast had shown that morning had so dismayed them, that they flatly refused to comply; begging him not to think of attempting it, as it would be at the risk of life or limb. But George was not to be daunted by such trifles; and seeing that his blood was up, and knowing that, when this was the case with him, he was not to be turned aside from his purpose, they at length yielded unwilling consent to his entreaties; and, giving him the required aid, he was soon mounted.

This was an insult the proud-spirited animal could not brook; and he began plunging and rearing in a manner so frightful to behold, that they who watched the struggle for mastery expected every moment to see the daring young rider hurled headlong to the ground. But he kept his seat unmoved and firm as an iron statue on an iron horse. At length, however, the horse, clinching the bit between his teeth, became for a time unmanageable, and sped away over the field on the wings of the wind; till, making a false step, he staggered and plunged, rallied again, staggered, and, with the red life-stream gushing from his nostrils, dropped down dead.

George sprang from the ground unharmed: but, when he saw the noble young animal stretched out smoking and bloody and lifeless before him, tears of pity filled his eyes; and still faster did they flow when he thought of the grief it would occasion his mother, when she should hear how her beautiful favorite had come to his end. His companions now rejoining him, they all, with sad misgiving in their hearts, returned to the house, where Mrs. Washington met them with a cheerful good-morning, and, when they had taken their seats at the breakfast-table, began talking with them in her usual lively and entertaining manner, until the dreaded question came: "Well, young gentlemen," said she, "have you seen any thing of my sorrel horse in your walks this morning?"

The boys looked at one another for some moments in silence, scarce knowing what answer to make. At last, George, to put an end to the painful suspense, said in a subdued voice, "Mother, the sorrel horse is dead." He then, in a few brief words, told her how it had all happened, and ended by entreating her forgiveness if he had offended; at the same time assuring her, that, in so doing, he had only thought of giving her a pleasant surprise.

When he first began his account of the mishap, a flush of anger rose to his mother's cheek; of which, however, there was not a trace to be seen by the time he had finished; and she answered, with something like an approving smile, "My son, as you have had the courage to come and tell me the truth at once, I freely forgive you: had you skulked away, I would have despised you, and been ashamed to own you as my son."

III.

PLAYING SOLDIER.

After the death of her husband, Mrs. Washington left the care and education of her son George, in no small measure, to the judgment and discretion of her step-son Lawrence, a young man of twenty-five, and lately married to Miss Fairfax. The love that had always existed between these two brothers was something beautiful indeed to behold,—the more so when we take into consideration the difference of fourteen years in their ages; and, now that their dear father was no more, this love grew all the more tender and strong, and George soon learned to look up to his eldest brother as to a second father.

Mr. Lawrence Washington, besides being a fine scholar and one of the most polished gentlemen of his day, was also a brave and able soldier; having served during the late Spanish war as a lieutenant under the great Admiral Vernon, in honor of whom he had named his fine estate on the Potomac, Mount Vernon.

At Mount Vernon, then, we find George spending by far the greater portion of his holidays; and here he often fell in with young officers, fellow-soldiers of his brother, to whom with eager ears he was wont to listen as they recounted their adventures, and told of hard-fought battles by land and sea with the roving pirates, or sea-robbers, and proud and vengeful Spaniards. These stories so fired his ardent young spirit, that he longed of all things to become a great soldier, that he might go forth to fight the enemies of his country, wherever they were to be found, and drive them from the face of the wide earth. To give these feelings some relief, he would muster his little school-fellows at play-time, and take them through the lessons of a military drill; showing them how to fire and fall back, how to advance and retreat, how to form in line of march, how to pitch their tents for a night's encampment, how to lay an Indian ambuscade, how to scale a wall, how to storm a battery; and, in short, forty other evolutions not to be found in any work on military tactics ever written, and at which old Wooden Leg, had he been there, would have shaken his cocked hat with a dubious look. Then dividing them into two opposing armies, with himself at the head of one, and the tallest boy of the school leading on the other, he would incite them to fight sham battles with wooden swords, wooden guns, snow-balls, and such other munitions of war as came most readily to hand; in which George, no matter what might be the odds against him, or what superior advantages the enemy might have in weapons or ground, was always sure to come off victorious.

He was a handsome boy, uncommonly tall, strong, and active for his age; could out-run, out-jump, out-ride any boy three years older than himself; and, in wrestling, there was not one in a hundred who could bring his back to the ground. Many stories are told of his wonderful strength; and the spot is still shown, where, when a boy, he stood on the banks of the Rappahannock River, and, at its widest part, threw a stone to the opposite side,—a feat that no one has been found able to perform since that day. It was said, that, a few years later, he stood under the Natural Bridge, and threw a silver dollar upon the top of it,—a height of two hundred and twenty feet; not less than that of Bunker-hill Monument, and more than double that of the tallest hickory that ever hailed down its ripened nuts upon your heads. Although there were none more studious than he in the schoolroom, yet he always took the keenest delight in every kind of active and manly sport, and was the acknowledged leader of the playground. But he had qualities of mind and heart far more desirable and meritorious than those of mere bodily activity and strength. Such was his love of truth, his strong sense of justice, and his clearness of judgment, that, when any dispute arose between his playmates, they always appealed to him to decide the difference between them, as willing to abide by his decision, and make it their law. Although he had the courage of a young lion, and was even more than a match in strength for many an older boy, he was never known to have a fight at school, nor elsewhere indeed, that I have ever heard; for such was the respect he ever showed to the feelings and wishes of others, that he never gave an insult, and, depend upon it, never received one.

The high ground of Mount Vernon commands a splendid view of the Potomac up and down for miles, where it makes a noble bend, and winds its shining course amidst verdant meadow-slopes and richly

The Farmer Boy and How He Became Commander-in-Chief

wooded hills. Now and then, in the course of the year, some noble ship, with all its sails outspread and gay banners fluttering to the breeze, might be seen moving down the majestic stream, hastening in its pride and strength to stem the billows of the mighty ocean. With the keenest of delight none but the young and daring mind can ever know, George, as he stood on the piazza in front of his brother's mansion, would watch them with wishful eyes, until a bend of the river hid their lofty masts behind the green tops of the yet more lofty hills between. Then would there awaken in his heart an earnest longing to become a sailor; to go forth in some gallant ship upon the face of the great deep; to visit those far-off countries, where he might behold with his own eyes those wonders he had read so much of in books. At such times, it may be, there would arise in his mind enchanting visions of some desert island, upon whose lonely rocky shores he might some day have the rare good fortune of being thrown by the angry billows, there to dwell, like another Robinson Crusoe, many, many years, with no other company than talking birds, skipping goats, and dancing cats, and, if so lucky, a good man Friday, to be rescued by his daring from the bloody clutches of the terrible cannibals.

Lawrence Washington was not long in discovering the thoughts that were uppermost in the mind of the adventurous boy; and, like the generous brother that he was, resolved that, should an opportunity offer, a wish so natural should be gratified. In a short time after, George being then about fourteen years of age, a British man-of-war moved up the Potomac, and cast anchor in full view of Mount Vernon. On board of this vessel his brother Lawrence procured him a midshipman's warrant, after having by much persuasion gained the consent of his mother; which, however, she yielded with much reluctance, and many misgivings with respect to the profession her son was about to choose. Not knowing how much pain all this was giving his mother, George was as near wild with delight as could well be with a boy of a nature so even and steady. Now, what had all along been but a waking dream was about to become a wide-awake reality. His preparations were soon made: already was his trunk packed, and carried on board the ship that was to bear him so far away from his native land; and nothing now remained but to bid farewell to the loved ones at home. But when he came and stood before his mother, dressed in his gay midshipman's uniform, so tall and robust in figure, so handsome in face, and so noble in look and gesture, the thought took possession of her mind, that, if she suffered him to leave her then, she might never see him more; and, losing her usual firmness and self-control, she burst into tears.

"Deeply do I regret, my dear son," said she, "to disappoint you in a wish you have so near at heart: but I find I cannot bring myself to give you up yet; for, young as you are, your aid and counsel have already become to me of the greatest service and comfort; and these little fatherless ones, now weeping around you, have learned to look up to you as their protector and guide. You know too little of the ways of the world, and are too young and inexperienced, to go forth to endure its hardships, and battle with its temptations, that lie in wait on every side to entrap the unwary, and lead them down to destruction. Without you, our home would be lonely indeed: then, for your mother's sake, and for the sake of these little ones, give up your darling scheme, for the present at least, that we may all be happy at home once more together."

Thus entreated, what could he do but yield consent to the wishes of a loving and prudent mother, and remain at home? where, in a few days, his noble self-denial was rewarded with a sweet contentment of mind that he could never have known had he left the dear ones in sorrow behind him, and gone forth to spend months and years upon the billows of the lonely seas. Surely a kind Heaven so ordered that the welfare and happiness of us Americans, and, it may be, that of the whole world, should be made to depend upon the promptings of a mother's love; for had the boy Washington realized this early dream, and gone forth in that gallant ship, he might have perished in the stormy deep, and we had never known the name we now love so much to praise and venerate. Or, by his distinguished abilities, he might have risen to become in time the Lord High Admiral of the British Navy; and, instead of being set apart to the salvation of his native land, might have been made an instrument to its destruction, impossible as such an event may now appear to us, with our knowledge of the glorious work he did perform when in the fulness of his strength and years, and accustomed as we are to behold in him our model of all that is great and virtuous in mankind.

IV.

"RULES OF BEHAVIOR."

For the five years following his father's death, George made his home at the house of his half-brother, Augustine Washington, at a considerable distance from his mother's, where he might have the benefit of a better school which that neighborhood afforded. His new schoolmaster was a Mr. Williams, a very worthy man; who, however, although he knew a vast deal more than Mr. Hobby, the poor old grave-digger, was far from being what we might call a first-rate scholar. But what his teacher lacked in learning, George made up in diligence, and the most judicious use of every means of self-improvement within his reach. And here, my dear children, let me remind you of a thing worthy of your remembrance through life, that success in the pursuit of knowledge depends far less upon the ability and skill of the teacher, than upon the industry, perseverance, and willing application of the learner.

Under the instruction of this, his second and last teacher, George got a little insight into English grammar, read some history, became well acquainted with geography, completely mastered arithmetic, and made handsome progress in geometry and trigonometry; which, as you must know, are higher branches of mathematics than arithmetic, and far more difficult to comprehend. In connection with the two latter, he studied surveying; by which is taught, as you must continue to bear in mind hereafter, the measurement of land.

When he had advanced so far in this study as to give him some idea of the proper use and handling of the chain and compass, the two principal instruments employed in this art, he began to put his knowledge into practice by taking surveys of the farms lying in the immediate neighborhood of his schoolhouse, and also of the lands belonging to the estate of Mount Vernon.

Assisted by his schoolmates, he would follow up, and measure off with the help of his long steel chain, the boundary lines between the farms, such as fences, roads, and watercourses; then those dividing the different parts of the same farm; determining at the same time, with the help of his compass, their various courses, their crooks and windings, and the angles formed at their points of meeting or intersection. This would enable him to get at the shape and size not only of each farm, but of every meadow, field, and wood composing it. This done, he would make a map or drawing on paper of the land surveyed, whereon would be clearly traced the lines dividing the different parts, with the name and number of acres of each attached; while, on the opposite page, he would write down the long and difficult tables of figures by which these results had been reached. All this he would execute with as much neatness and accuracy as if it had been left with him to decide thereby some gravely disputed land-claim.

To qualify himself for the management of business affairs upon reaching the age of manhood, he would copy off into a blank-book every form or instrument of writing he would meet with; such as deeds, wills, notes of hand, bills of exchange, receipts, bonds, land-warrants, &c., &c. And, what was still more remarkable in a boy of thirteen, he wrote down, under the head of what he called "Rules of Behavior in Company and Conversation," such wise maxims, and lines of wholesome advice, as he would pick up from time to time in the course of his reading or observation, to aid him in forming habits of industry, politeness, and morality. Some of these rules, your Uncle Juvinell, with an eye mainly to your well-being, will repeat to you; for, when but a boy, he got them by heart, well knowing, that, without some such aid, he would find it hard, if not impossible, to so order his walks through life as to win and deserve the esteem and confidence of his fellow-men, as well as the blessing and approbation of his Maker. And now that he has reached the evening of his days, and is well assured that the daily observance of these rules has made him a wiser, a better, and a happier man, he would most earnestly advise all his friends, great or small, but especially small, be they boys or girls, to pursue the like course, if they would be favored of Heaven in the like manner. Here they are:—

"1. Every action in company ought to be with some sign of respect to those present.

"2. In the presence of others, sing not to yourself with a humming noise, nor drum with your fingers or feet.

"3. Speak not when others speak, sit not when others stand, speak not when you should hold your peace, walk not when others stop.

"4. Turn not your back to others, especially in speaking; jog not the table or desk on which another reads or writes; lean not on any one.

"5. Be not a flatterer; neither play with any one that delights not to be played with.

"6. Show not yourself glad at the misfortune of another, though he were your enemy.

"7. It is good manners to prefer them to whom we speak before ourselves, especially if they be above us; with whom in no sort ought we to begin.

"8. Strive not with your superiors in an argument, but always submit your judgment to others with modesty.

"9. Undertake not to teach your equal in the art himself professes; for it is immodest and presumptuous.

"10. When a man does all he can, though it succeeds not well, blame not him that did it.

"11. Before you advise or find fault with any one, consider whether it ought to be in public or in private, presently or at some other time, in what terms to do it; and, in reproving, show no signs of anger, but do it with sweetness and mildness.

"12. Take all advice thankfully, in what time or place soever given; but afterwards, not being blamable, take a time or place convenient to let him know it that gave it.

"13. Mock not in jest at any thing of importance: if you deliver any thing witty and pleasant, abstain from laughing thereat yourself.

"14. Wherein you reprove another, be unblamable yourself; for example is better than precept.

"15. Use no reproachful language against any one; neither curse nor revile.

"16. Be not hasty to believe flying reports to the injury of any.

"17. In your apparel, be modest, and endeavor to accommodate yourself to nature, rather than to procure admiration; keep to the fashion of your equals, such as are civil and orderly, with respect to time and places.

"18. Play not the peacock, looking everywhere about you to see if you be well decked, if your shoes fit well, if your pantaloons sit neatly, and clothes handsomely.

"19. Associate yourself with men of good quality, if you esteem your reputation; for it is better to be alone than in bad company.

"20. Let your conversation be without malice or envy, for it is a sign of a kindly and commendable nature; and, in all causes of passion, admit reason to govern.

"21. Be not immodest in urging a friend to make known a secret.

"22. Utter not base and frivolous things amongst grave and learned men, nor very difficult questions or subjects among the ignorant, nor things hard to believe.

"23. Speak not of doleful things in time of mirth, nor at the table; speak not of melancholy things, as death and wounds; and, if others mention them, change, if you can, the discourse. Tell not your dreams but to your intimate friend.

"24. Break not a jest, when none take pleasure in mirth; laugh not loud, nor at all, without occasion; deride no man's misfortune, though there seem to be some cause.

"25. Speak not injurious words, neither in jest nor earnest; scoff at none, although they give occasion.

"26. Seek not to lessen the merits of others; neither give more than due praise.

"27. Go not thither where you know not whether you shall be welcome. Give not advice without being asked; and, when desired, do it briefly.

"28. Reprove not the imperfections of others; for that belongs to parents, masters, and superiors.

"29. Gaze not on the marks or blemishes of others, and ask not how they came. What you may speak in secret to your friend, deliver not before others.

"30. Think before you speak; pronounce not imperfectly, nor bring out your words too hastily, but orderly and distinctly.

"31. When another speaks, be attentive yourself, and disturb not the audience. If any hesitate in his words, help him not nor prompt him without being desired; interrupt him not nor answer him until his speech be ended.

"32. Treat with men at right times about business, and whimper not in the company of others.

"33. Be not in haste to relate news, if you know not the truth thereof.

"34. Be not curious to know the affairs of others; neither approach those that speak in private.

"35. Undertake not what you cannot perform, but be careful to keep your promise.

"36. When your masters or superiors talk to anybody, hearken not, nor speak or laugh.

"37. Speak not evil of the absent; for it is unjust.

"38. Make no show of taking delight in your victuals; feed not with greediness; cut your food with a knife, and lean not on the table; neither find fault with what you eat.

"39. Be not angry at the table, whatever happens; and, if you have reason to be so, show it not, but put on a cheerful face, especially if there be strangers; for good humor makes of one dish a feast.

"40. If you speak of God or his attributes, let it be seriously, in reverence; and honor and obey your parents.

"41. Let your recreations be manful, not sinful.

"42. Labor to keep in your breast that little spark of celestial fire called conscience."

Now, does it not strike you, my dear children, as being most truly wonderful that it should have ever entered the mind of a boy of thirteen to lay down for his own guidance and self-improvement such rules and principles as these I have just repeated? It certainly must. And yet when I tell you that he strictly adhered to them through life, and squared his conduct by them daily, you will, no doubt, think it quite unreasonable that he could have been other than the good and great man he was.

These writings I have mentioned filled several quires of paper; and together with his business papers, letters, journals, and account-books, written later in life, and with the same neatness and precision, are still preserved at Mount Vernon with pious care; and are even now to be seen by those who go on pilgrimages to that sacred spot, although, since many of them were penned, more than a hundred years have come and gone.

And thus, my children, you have seen young Washington, at an age when most boys are wasting their precious hours in idle sports, seeking to acquire those habits of industry, punctuality, and method, which afterwards enabled him so to economize time and labor as to do with ease and expedition what others did with difficulty and tardiness. You have seen him making the best use of the slender means within his reach for storing his mind with those treasures of knowledge, and schooling his heart in the daily practice of those exalted virtues, which, after a life well spent and work well done, make good his title to the name he bears,—the greatest and the wisest of human kind.

At last, the day came when George was to leave school for ever; and a day of sorrow it was to his school-fellows, who parted from him with many an affectionate wish, and, as we are told, even with tears;

so greatly had he endeared himself to them by his noble disposition, gentle manners, and earnest desire to do as he would be done by, which appeared in all his words and actions. In these regrets, Mr. Williams, his worthy schoolmaster, also shared; and it gave him in after-life, when his little George had become the great Washington, the most heartfelt pleasure to say, that it had never been his privilege to teach another pupil who could at all compare with him for diligence in application, aptitude in learning, docility of disposition, manly generosity, courage, and truth.

V.

IN THE WILDERNESS.

Extending from the Rappahannock to the Potomac, and stretching away beyond the Blue Ridge far into the Alleghany Mountains, there lay at this time an immense tract of forest land, broken only here and there by a little clearing, in the midst of which stood the rude log-cabin of some hardy backwoodsman. This large body of land—the largest, indeed, ever owned by any one man in Virginia—was the property of a great English nobleman named Lord Fairfax, an old bachelor of eccentric habits and strange opinions, but of a highly cultivated understanding, and, when it so pleased him, of polite and elegant address. His stature was lofty,—far above that of the common run of men. He was a keen sportsman, had a fund of whimsical humor, and, in his odd way, showed himself possessed of a kindly and generous heart; sometimes making a tenant or poor friend the present of a large farm, without requiring any thing in return but a haunch of venison or a fat wild turkey for his next Christmas dinner.

Having heard that settlements were being made in the most fertile valleys of his wild domain, he had lately come over from the mother-country to inquire into the matter, and make suitable provision against any future encroachments of the kind upon his rights. He now beheld his forest possessions for the first time; and so charmed was he with the wild beauty of the scenery, and so won over by enticing visions of fishing and hunting, conjured up by the sight of the waving woods and running streams, that he resolved to leave his native land for ever, and take up his abiding-place for the rest of his days amid those leafy solitudes. Accordingly, he betook himself, with all his negro servants (numbering one hundred and fifty), and a few white dependants, to the beautiful Valley of the Shenandoah, lying between the Blue Ridge and the Alleghany Mountains; where he soon cleared a large plantation, and built thereon a house, to which he gave the name of Greenway Court.

From that time forward, this became his fixed abode; but, as he had more land than a thousand men could put to any good use, he was quite willing to dispose of all, except what lay for a few miles immediately around Greenway Court, at reasonable rates, to such honest persons as were willing to buy it and make it their future home. But, in order that no misunderstanding might arise hereafter between the parties concerned with respect to the boundary-line and number of acres bought and sold, it was necessary, in the first place, to have the land surveyed, and divided into lots of convenient sizes for farms.

Now, you must know that, old Lord Fairfax was a distant relative of Mrs. Lawrence Washington, and had, as a natural consequence, often met our George at Mount Vernon; and so struck was he with the manly bearing, high character, good sense, and mathematical skill, of the fair-haired, blue-eyed youth, that he offered him, young as he was, the place of surveyor of all his vast lands. Being the son of a widowed mother, and earnestly desirous of aiding her all in his power, and earning for himself an honest independence, George was but too happy to accept of the offer; and the necessary arrangements were soon made. Having provided himself with all things needful for the new enterprise,—such as a horse, a rifle, a blanket, and a steel chain and compass,—he set out, at the head of a small party of hunters and backwoodsmen, upon this his first considerable field of labor, early in the spring of 1748, just one month from the completion of his sixteenth year.

They were soon, in the depths of the wilderness, miles beyond the most distant frontier settlements. The snows of winter that still lingered on the mountains, warmed by the softer airs of early spring, had melted so rapidly of late as to swell the forest streams to a degree that rendered their fording often difficult, and even sometimes dangerous. Now and then, coming to a stream which had overflowed its banks, the little party would be obliged to construct a raft of logs, roughly lashed together with grape-vines, upon which they could push to the opposite side, without getting their baggage wet, and, at the same time, compel their horses to swim along behind. Their way was often obstructed by the trunks and branches of fallen trees, thickets tangled and dense and thorny, huge and rugged rocks, and treacherous swamps, covered with long, green grass, into which the horses, stepping unawares, would suddenly plunge up to the saddle-girths in water and mire.

For some time, they lodged in wigwams or huts, rudely framed of poles, and covered with the bark of trees; which served the purpose well enough when the weather was dry and still, but were often beaten down and overturned by the winds and rains when their shelter was most needed. After two or three of these rickety shanties had been tumbled about their heads, to the no small risk of life or limb, they wisely concluded to abandon them, and sleep in the open air, with the twinkling stars above them, the gray old trees around them, and the damp, cold ground beneath them, with nothing between but their good blankets, and the dead, dry leaves of autumn heaped together; and lucky was he who got the place nearest the fire, or could put the mossy trunk of a fallen tree between him and the biting blast, or, better still, could boast a bearskin for his bed. A little before sunset, they would halt for the night in some sheltered spot, convenient to a running stream; where, turning their horses loose to graze till morning, they would build a cheerful fire of the dry brushwood close at hand, and prepare their evening meal, which they would eat with a keenness of appetite known only to the tired and hungry hunter. Each man was his own cook; their food consisting chiefly of venison and wild turkey their rifles procured them, and fish drawn from the neighboring brook, which they would broil on the glowing coals, fastened to a forked stick instead of a spit, and then eat it from a maple chip, instead of a dish. If the season permitted them to add to this a hatful of berries that grew on the sunny side of the hill, or acorns from the mountain-oak, or nuts from the hickory-tree, or, more delicious still, plums, persimmons, and pawpaws, that grew in the more open parts of the woods, they made of it a dainty feast indeed.

Now and then, in the course of this rambling life in the wilderness, they met with roving bands of skin-clad Indians, either as warriors out upon the war-path against some distant tribe, or as hunters roaming the forest in quest of game. One evening, late, as our little party of surveyors were about to encamp for the night, they spied through the trees the glimmering light of a large fire on the top of a

The Farmer Boy and How He Became Commander-in-Chief

far-off hill. Curious to know who, besides themselves, could be in that lonely place, they determined to go thither before stopping; and, guided by the light, reached ere long the spot, where they found a small squad of Indian hunters, resting themselves after the fatigues of the day's chase. They seemed to be in high good humor, as if the hunt had gone well with them that day; and, being in this mood, extended a true Indian welcome to the new-comers; setting before them, with open-handed hospitality, heaps of parched corn, and their choicest bits of venison, wild turkey, bear's meat, and fish. Supper ended, the pipe of peace and good-will passed from mouth to mouth, as a pledge that all should go on well between them; after which the Indians, for the further entertainment of their white guests, and as a more marked manner of showing their respect, set about preparing themselves for a war-dance.

In the first place, they cleared the ground around the fire of chunks and brushwood, and other obstructions that might hinder the free play of their feet and legs in the performance. Then the two musicians began to put in order and tune their instruments: that is to say, one of them filled a camp-kettle half full of water, over which he tightly stretched a raw-hide, and, tapping it twice or thrice with a stick, drew forth a hollow, smothered sound therefrom, by way of giving to those not in the secret a hint that this was to be their drum; while the other made a rattle by putting a few bullets or pebbles into a hard, dry gourd of monstrous size, to the handle of which he fastened a horse's tail, not so much to improve its tone perhaps, as to give it a more finished appearance.

These simple preparations soon completed, a tall warrior, grimly painted as if for battle, advanced a few paces into the circle, and, squatting upon his haunches, fixed his eyes for several moments with a hard, stony look upon nothing whatever, till the first tap of the drum and the first jerk of the rattle, when he suddenly leaped up, with a deafening yell that made the old woods ring again, and began capering about in the most astonishing manner, causing such a commotion among the dry leaves and dead twigs as made it appear that a little whirlwind had all at once been let loose among them. Another soon followed, and got up a similar sensation among the dry leaves and dead twigs on his own private account; while a third, springing into the circle, did the same; and so on, until at last the whole party were hot in the dance. Some brandished their scalping-knives, some flourished their tomahawks, some waved aloft the scalps of their enemies taken in battle; all yelling the while, and all making horrible faces. And warmer and warmer they waxed in the dance, and round and round they went; now up in the air, now down on the ground; jumping and kicking, yelping and barking, spinning and whirling, yelling and howling, like a pack of hobgoblins and imps on a spree. The hollow woods gave back the barbarous din in a thousand obstreperous echoes; and afar off, from the depths of the lonely forest glens, might have been heard, had not the attention of the spectators been otherwise engaged, the answering howl of the hungry wolves.

After some time spent in this outlandish amusement, without any previous notice whatever, plump down they sat, and, in a minute, were smoking their pipes with as much gravity and composure as if they had just come in from a gentle promenade with their wives and children along the banks of a smooth and tranquil river. It was a sight, once seen, never to be forgotten. At first, George and his friends had looked on with open-eyed amazement; but, before the dance was ended, the whole scene appeared to them so comical, that they had need of all their self-control to keep a sober countenance, so as not to give offence to their savage entertainers.

VI.

THE YOUNG SURVEYOR.

It was a glorious region of stately woods, fertile valleys, clear running streams, and lofty mountains, where our young surveyor, with the exception of the winter months, spent the next three years of his life. At first, not being accustomed to such severe privations and exposure, it had gone rather hard with him: but he soon became inured to them; and it was, no doubt, to this rough experience in the wilderness, that he owed, in large measure, his uncommon vigor and activity of body, and that firm reliance on the resources of his own mind, which enabled him to endure and overcome those hardships, trials, and difficulties which beset him throughout the greater portion of his after-life. This severe training was also of another advantage to him, in making him perfectly familiar with all that region, in whose dark retreats and rugged wilds he learned, a few years later, his first hard lessons in the art of war.

With all its privations, it was a life he loved to lead; for it afforded him the means of an independent support: and a happy boy was he, when first he wrote his mother that he was earning from fifteen to twenty dollars for every day he worked. Besides this, the beauty and grandeur of Nature's works, everywhere visible around him, awakened in him feelings of the truest delight; and he would sometimes spend the better part of a summer's day in admiring the tall and stately trees, whose spreading branches were his only shelter from the dews of heaven, and heat of noonday. At night, after supper, when his companions would be talking over the adventures of the day just past, or laughing boisterously at some broad joke repeated for the hundredth time, or would be joining their voices in the chorus of some rude woodland song, our young surveyor would be sitting a little apart on the trunk of a fallen tree, pencil and paper before him, calculating with a grave countenance, and by the ruddy light of a blazing pine-knot, the results of the day's labor. With no other companionship than that of the wild Indians he fell in with from time to time, and the rude, unlettered hunters around him, he must needs turn for society to the thoughts that stirred within his own mind. Often would he withdraw himself from the noisy mirth of his companions, and, climbing to some lofty mountain-top, spend hours and hours rapt in the contemplation of the wild and varied region, smiling in life and beauty far, far beneath him. At such times, we can imagine his countenance lit up with a sacred joy, and his soul rising in praise and thanksgiving to the great Father, who, in love and wisdom, made this glorious world for the good and happiness of all that dwell therein.

Now and then, for the sake of a refreshing change, he would leave the wilderness behind him, with all its toils and dangers, and betake him to Greenway Court, the woodland home of old Lord Fairfax, with whom he had become a great favorite, and was ever a welcome guest. Here he would spend a few weeks in the most agreeable manner you can well imagine; for the old lord, being a man of some learning and extensive reading, had collected, in the course of a long life, a large library of the best and rarest books, from which, during these three years, George derived great pleasure and much valuable information. Besides this, a keener fox-hunter than this odd old bachelor was not to be found in all the Old Dominion; and, for the full enjoyment of this sport, he always kept a pack of hounds of the purest English blood. At the first peep of dawn, the cheerful notes of the hunter's horn, and the deep-mouthed baying of the fox-hounds, filling the neighboring woods with their lively din, would call our young surveyor from his slumbers to come and join in the sports of the morning. Waiting for no second summons, he would be up and out in a trice, and mounted by the side of the merry old lord; when, at a signal wound on the bugle, the whole party would dash away, pell-mell, helter-skelter, over the hills and through the woods, up the hills and down them again, across the brooks and along the winding river; hunters and horses hard on the heels of the hounds, hounds hard on the heels of poor Renard, and poor Renard cutting, cutting away for dear life.

During the three years thus employed, George made his home at Mount Vernon, it being nearer and more convenient to his field of labor; but, as often as his business would permit, he would go on a visit to his mother at the old homestead on the Rappahannock, whither, as I should have told you before now, his father had removed when he was but three or four years old. These were precious opportunities, ever improved by him, of extending to her that aid in the management of her family affairs, which to receive from him was her greatest pleasure, as well as his truest delight to give.

About this time, he formed a habit of writing down in a diary or day-book such facts and observations as seemed to him worthy of note, by which means he would be enabled to fix firmly in his mind whatever might prove of use to him at a future day. This is a most excellent habit; and I would earnestly advise all young persons, desirous of increasing their stock of knowledge, to form it as soon as they begin the study of grammar and can write a good round hand. The following is a specimen of this diary, written by him at the age of sixteen, as you will see by the date therein given:—

"March 13th, 1748.—Rode to his lordship's (Lord Fairfax's) quarter. About four miles higher up the Shenandoah, we went through most beautiful groves of sugar-trees, and spent the better part of the day in admiring the trees and richness of the land.

"14th.—We sent our baggage to Capt. Hite's, near Fredericktown; and went ourselves down the river about sixteen miles (the land exceedingly rich all the way, producing abundance of grain, hemp, and tobacco), in order to lay off some land on Cole's Marsh and Long Marsh.

"15th.—Worked hard till night, and then returned. After supper, we were lighted into a room; and I, not being so good a woodsman as the rest, stripped myself very orderly, and went into the bed, as they called it; when, to my surprise, I found it to be nothing but a little straw matted together, without sheet or any thing else, but only one threadbare blanket, with double its weight of vermin, I was glad to get up and put on my clothes, and lie as my companions did. Had we not been very tired, I am sure we should not have slept much that night. I made a promise to sleep so no more; choosing rather to sleep in the open air, before a fire.

"18th.—We travelled to Thomas Berwick's on the Potomac, where we found the river exceedingly high, by reason of the great rains that had fallen among the Alleghanies. They told us it would not be fordable for several days; it being now six feet higher than usual, and rising. We agreed to stay till Monday. We this day called to see the famed Warm Springs. We camped out in the field this night.

"20th.—Finding the river not much abated, we in the evening swam our horses over to the Maryland side.

"21st.—We went over in a canoe, and travelled up the Maryland side all day, in a continued rain, to Col. Cresap's, over against the mouth of the South Branch, about forty miles from the place of starting in the morning, and over the worst road, I believe, that ever was trod by man or beast."

In this diary, he also entered such items as these,—the number of acres of each lot of land surveyed, the quality of the soil, the growth of plants and trees, the height of the hills, the extent of the valleys, and the length, breadth, and course of the streams. From the items thus collected, he would draw the materials for the reports it was his duty to submit, from time to time, for examination, to his patron or employer; and such was the clearness, brevity, and exactness displayed therein, and such the industry, skill, and fidelity with which he performed his toilsome and difficult task, that the generous old lord not only rewarded him handsomely for his services, but continued to cherish for him through life a truly fatherly affection.

In after-years, Washington was wont to turn with peculiar fondness to this period of his life, as perhaps affording the only leisure he had ever known for sentimental musings, and the indulgence of what fancy he may have had in those bright visions of future happiness, fame, or enterprise; to which all men are more or less given during the immature years of youth. This, to my mind, is to be easily enough accounted for, if we but ascribe it to a certain little circumstance; concerning which, as it exercised no small influence on his mind at the time, I will now tell you all that is known, and, it may be, more than ever can be known with possible certainty.

From a letter written by him at the age of fifteen, and also from some sad and plaintive verses of his own composition found in his copybook, we learn that the boy, who should grow to become the greatest man that ever made this glorious world of ours more glorious with his wise precepts and virtuous example, was at this time a victim of the tender passion called *love*, of which most of you little folks as yet know nothing but the four letters that spell the word.

The object of this early attachment was a damsel, of whom nothing certain is known, as her name, from the fact of its never being repeated above a whisper, has not come down to our day, but who was called by him in his confidential correspondence the Lowland Beauty. As he had none of that self-assurance which lads of his age are apt to mistake for pluck or spirit, he never ventured to make known the secret of this passion to the object thereof; and it is probable, that we, even at the big end of a hundred years, are wiser as to this tender passage of his life than was ever the young lady herself. Not having the courage to declare the sentiments that warmed his breast, he wisely resolved to banish them from his mind altogether; and this, I will venture to say, was one reason why he so readily accepted of old Lord Fairfax's offer, and was willing for so long a time to make his abiding-place in the wilderness. But it was months, and even years, before he could get the better of his weakness, if such it could be justly called; for a wilderness, let me tell you (and I hope the hint will not be lost on my little friends), is the last place in the world, that a man, or a boy either, should take to, as the readiest means of ridding himself of such troublesome feelings. No wonder, then, that our young surveyor was grave and thoughtful beyond his years; and that the lonely forest, with its ever-changing beauties and wild seclusion, viewed through the bewitched eyes of love, should have had greater charms for him than the noisy, bustling haunts of men. That you may have a more distinct idea of the appearance of Washington at the time of which we are speaking, your Uncle Juvinell will conjure up, from the lingering lights and shadows of his dull old fancy, a little picture, to be gilded anew by your bright young fancies, and hung up in that loftiest chamber of your memory which you are wont to adorn with your portraits of the good and great men and women who have blessed the earth, and of whom we love so much to read and hear.

It is a summer morning, and the eastern mountains fling their shadows long and huge across the lonesome valleys. Our little party of surveyors, having spent the night on the summits of one of the less lofty peaks of the Blue Ridge, are slowly descending its shrubby skies to the more densely wooded parts of the wilderness below, of whose waste fertility many a broad tract have they yet to explore, and many a mile of boundary-line have chain and compass yet to measure and determine. Still lingering on the summit far above, as loath to quit the contemplation of the splendid prospect seen from thence, stands a tall youth of eighteen, with his right arm thrown across his horse's neck, and his left hand grasping his compass-staff. He is clad in a buckskin hunting-shirt, with leggins and moccasons of the same material,—the simple garb of a backwoodsman, and one that well becomes him now, as in perfect keeping with the wildness of the surrounding scenery; while in his broad leathern belt are stuck his long hunting-knife and Indian tomahawk. In stature he is much above most youths of the same age: he is of a handsome and robust form, with high and strong but smooth features, light-brown hair, large blue eyes,—not brilliant, but beaming with a clear and steady light, as if a soul looked through them that knew no taint of vice or meanness,—and a countenance all glorious with a truth and courage, modest gentleness, and manly self-reliance; and as he thus lingers on that lonely mountain-height, glorified as it were with the fresh pure light of the newly risen sun, with head uncovered and looks reverent, he seems in holy communion with his Maker, to whom, in the tender, guileless years of childhood, a pious mother taught him to kneel, morning and evening, in prayer, thanksgiving, and adoration.

Anon, his morning devotions ended, he turns to take, ere following his companions down the mountain, another view of the varied panorama spread out far beneath him, the chief feature of which is a valley, surpassing in beauty and fertility any that that summer's sun will shine on ere reaching his golden gateway in the west. Through this valley, glimmering, half seen, half hid among the waving woods, runs a river, with many a graceful bend, so beautiful, that, in the far-away years of the past, some long-forgotten tribe of Indians called it Shenandoah, or Shining Daughter of the Stars; a name that still lingers like a sweet echo among the mountains. And as the eyes of the young surveyor slowly range the wide prospect from point to point, and take in miles and miles of beauty at a single stretch of view, there is a look in them as if he would recall some pleasing dream of the night, which he would now fain bring forth, though but a dream, to refine and elevate the thoughts wherewith his mind must needs be occupied throughout the day. He is familiar with every feature of the landscape before him: he knows each shady dell and sunny hill, and every grassy slope and winding stream; for there he has made his home this many a day. He has seen it all a thousand times, and each time with renewed delight. But now it has a glory not all its own, nor borrowed from the morning sun, but from the first warm light of youthful love that burns in his heart for his Lowland Beauty.

VII.

FIRST MILITARY APPOINTMENT.

About this time, the Indians inhabiting that vast region extending from the Ohio River to the great lakes of the north, secretly encouraged and aided by the French, began to show signs of hostility, and threatened the western borders of Virginia, Pennsylvania, and New York, with all the dismal horrors of their bloody and wasting warfare. The alarm spread rapidly from the frontier even to the Atlantic coast, till the whole country was awakened to the sense of the impending danger.

To put the Province of Virginia in a better posture of defence, the governor thereof, Robert Dinwiddie, besides other measures, divided it into four grand military districts. Over each of these he placed what is called an adjutant-general, whose duty it was to organize and train the militia, instruct the officers in matters touching the art and science of war, to review the different companies when on parade, and to inspect their arms and accoutrements, and see that they were kept ready for use at a moment's warning.

The energy, fidelity, and soundness of judgment, that young Washington had lately shown while acting as surveyor, had won for him a name in the colony; and, becoming known to Governor Dinwiddie, he was appointed by that gentleman adjutant-general of the Northern district; receiving along with his commission the rank of major, which entitled him to the salary of seven hundred and fifty dollars a year. You have already seen what great delight he took in martial exercises when a school-boy; and, now that he was to become a soldier in the true sense of the term, you will not be surprised to learn that this appointment was altogether agreeable to his present taste and inclinations. To show his deep sense of the honor done him, and the trust and confidence reposed in him, he determined to perform his work well and faithfully as far as in him lay.

The Farmer Boy and How He Became Commander-in-Chief

The better to qualify himself for the duties of his office, he placed himself under the instruction of his brother Lawrence, and other officers living in that part of the province, who had served under Admiral Vernon during the late Spanish war. These gentlemen, besides giving him the benefit of their experience and observation, placed in his hands the best works on military science then in use; from which he learned the various modes of training militia, the different manœuvres of an army on the field of battle, and their management while on the line of march, together with the most approved plans of building forts, throwing up intrenchments and redoubts, and the construction of other works of defence, whether of wood or earth or stone. At the same time, he also made himself acquainted with the handling and design of many weapons and engines of war; and under the instruction of Capt. Van Braam, a Dutch fencing-master, he became very skilful in the use of the sword. Thus Mount Vernon, from being the quiet mansion of a country gentleman, was now, in a manner, converted into a military school; and the youth, who but a few years before, as he strolled among its verdant retreats, had, in honor of his Lowland Beauty, made his first and only attempt of putting his thoughts and feelings in verse, was, at the early age of nineteen, called upon to discharge those stern duties which men of age and experience alone are generally thought able to perform. The district allotted to Major Washington (for so we must now call him) consisted of several large counties, each of which the duties of his office obliged him to visit from time to time; and such was the energy and spirit he carried into his work, and such ability did he display, and such was the manliness and dignified courtesy with which he deported himself on all occasions, that he soon completely won the confidence and affections of both officers and men, who were inspired by his example to still greater zeal and patriotism in the service of their country.

But these labors, so agreeable to one of his age and ardent spirit, were now interrupted for several months. His brother Lawrence, who had always been of a delicate constitution, was now thought to be in the last stages of consumption, and was advised by his physicians to betake himself to the West Indies, where he might yet, perhaps, find some relief in the warmer suns and milder airs of those beautiful islands. As he would have need of cheerful company and gentle and careful nursing, he took with him his favorite brother George; and, embarking from Alexandria, was soon out upon the shining billows of the deep-blue sea, in quest of that health he was never again to find. Their place of destination was the charming little Island of Barbadoes, where, after a somewhat stormy voyage, they arrived in safety.

While here, Major Washington had an attack of small-pox, which handled him rather severely; and for some time he was thought to be in a dangerous condition. But in a few weeks, by dint of careful nursing, joined to the natural vigor of his constitution, he got the better of this frightful malady; and, when he was completely restored, not a disfiguring trace of it remained.

During his sojourn here, he still continued his habit of writing down in a journal whatever of importance or interest came under his observation; in which, among other items, we find such as the following,—the speed of the ship in which they sailed; the direction of the winds; some account of a storm that overtook them on their voyage; the cities, ships, forts, and military strength of the Island of Barbadoes; its products; manners and customs of the people, and the laws and government under which they lived. By this means, contributing as it did to habits of close and accurate observation, he impressed the more strongly upon his memory such facts as might prove of use to him at a future day.

Our two Virginians, during the three or four months of their stay on the island, were treated with much courtesy and hospitality by the inhabitants. But neither the genial climate of the region, nor the kindly hospitality of the people, was enough to restore that health and strength to the invalid for which he had come so far and hoped so long.

Feeling that his end was drawing nigh, Lawrence Washington resolved to hasten home, that he might have the melancholy satisfaction of spending his last moments in the midst of his family and friends. He had scarcely returned to Mount Vernon, and bid a fond farewell to the loved ones there, when the angel of death summoned him to take another and a longer voyage, in quest of immortality, to be found in the islands of the blest, that smile in never-fading beauty on the bosom of the eternal sea.

Thus, at the early age of thirty-four, died Lawrence Washington, one of the most amiable and accomplished gentlemen of his day. He left behind him an affectionate wife, a sweet little daughter, a devoted brother, and many a loving friend, to mourn his loss. In his will, he bequeathed his fine estate of Mount Vernon and all else that he possessed to his brother George; on condition, however, that his wife should have the use of it during her lifetime, and that his daughter should die without children to inherit it. The daughter did not reach the years of maidenhood; and, the mother surviving but a few years, George was left in the undivided possession of a large and handsome property; and, in a worldly point of view, his fortune was really already made. But, for all that, he long and deeply mourned the death of this much loved and valued brother, who had been to him father and friend ever since that first great sorrow of his childhood, when he became a widow's son and a widow's blessing.

And thus, my little children, I have told you the story of this great and good man's life from his years of infancy up to those of early manhood. I have dwelt at greater length upon this period of his life than perhaps any other historian, and have told you some things that you might look for elsewhere in vain. In my treatment of this part of the subject, it has been my chief aim and earnest desire to impress upon your opening minds this one great truth,—that, if you would be good and wise in your manhood, you must begin, now in early youth, to put forth all your powers, and use all the means within your reach, to store your mind with useful knowledge, and direct your thoughts and actions in the ways of truth and virtue, industry and sobriety. The boy Washington did all this; and, ere we have done, you shall see the glorious results of such a good beginning. Be like him in your youth,—patient and diligent, loving and dutiful, truthful and prayerful; that you may be like him in the fulness of years,—esteemed and beloved, happy and good, useful and wise.

VIII.

IMPORTANT EXPLANATIONS.

When Uncle Juvinell had finished this part of his story, he paused, and with a beaming face looked round upon his little circle of listeners. Two or three of the youngest had long since fallen asleep; and Master Ned, having heard the story of the little hatchet, had stolen quietly away to the cabin, just to see how "black daddy" was getting along with his sled. Having waited till it was finished, he had, for his own private amusement, taken it to a nice hillside, and was now coasting on it all alone by the light of a good-humored, dish-faced moon. The other children had listened with great interest and attention to the story, and were still sitting with their eyes bent earnestly on the fire, whose great bright eye had by this time grown a little red, and was winking in a slow and sleepy way, as if it were saying, "Well done, Uncle Juvinell,—very well done indeed. I have been listening very attentively, and quite approve of all you have said, especially all that about the wooden-legged schoolmaster, the little hatchet, the sorrel horse, the Indian war-dance, and the Lowland Beauty, not to mention those wise maxims and wholesome moral precepts you brought in so aptly. All of it is very fine and very good, and just to my liking. But I am thinking it is high bed-time for these little folks."

Uncle Juvinell was much gratified to see how deeply interested the children were in what he had been telling them; and in a little while he called upon them to let him know how they all liked it. Laura said that it was very nice; Ella, that it was charming; Daniel, that it was quite as interesting as Plutarch's Lives; Willie, that it was even more so than "Robinson Crusoe;" and Bryce, that it was very good, but he would have liked it better had Uncle Juvinell told them more about the Indians. Just then, Master Charlie awoke from a comfortable nap of an hour or two, having dropped asleep shortly after the sorrel horse dropped dead; and, to make believe that he had been as wide awake as a weasel from the very start, began asking such a string of questions as seemed likely to have no end. After a droll jumbling of Washington with Jack the Giant-killer, old Lord Fairfax with

The Farmer Boy and How He Became Commander-in-Chief

Bluebeard, poor old Hobby, the wooden-legged schoolmaster, with the Roving Red Robber, he at last so far got the better of his sleepy senses as to know what he would be driving at; when he said, "Uncle Juvinell, did his father let him keep his little hatchet after he had cut the cherry-tree?"

"History, my little nephew," replied his uncle with a sober countenance, "does not inform us whether he did or not; but you may be quite sure that he did, well knowing that a little boy who would choose rather to take a whipping than tell a lie, or suffer another to be punished for an offence he had himself committed, would never be guilty the second time of doing that wherein he had once been forbidden."

"What became of black Jerry after he turned a somerset in the snow, and went rolling over and over down the hill?" Charlie went on.

"Jerry, I am happy to say," replied his uncle, "was so won over by the kindness and noble self-devotion of his brave little master, that he made up his mind to mend his ways from that very moment; and in a short time, from having been the worst, became the best behaved negroling to be found on either side of the Rappahannock, for more than a hundred miles up and down."

"What is a negroling?" inquired Master Charlie, as if bent on sifting this matter to the very bottom.

"A negroling," replied Uncle Juvinell with a smile, "is to a full-grown negro what a gosling is to a full-grown goose. Now, can you tell me what it is?"

"A gosling negro, I suppose," was Charlie's answer; and then he asked, "Did old Hobby go on teaching school after little George left him?"

"Of course he did," answered his uncle; "but, you may depend upon it, he never took another scholar as far as the single rule of three." Then, winking slyly at two or three of the older children, he continued: "This worthy schoolmaster lived to the good old age of ninety-nine; when, feeling that his earthly pilgrimage was drawing to a close, he for the last time hung up his big cocked hat on the accustomed peg, and for the last time unscrewed his wooden, leg, and set it in its accustomed corner; then, like a good Christian, laid him down to die in peace, giving thanks to Heaven with his last breath that it had fallen to his lot to teach the great George Washington his A B C's and the multiplication-table."

This made Master Charlie look very grave and thoughtful, so that he asked no more questions for the rest of the night.

Then Daniel, the young historian, who, having his mind occupied with more weighty matters, had been listening with some impatience while the above confab was going on, begged that his uncle would tell him what was meant by a midshipman's warrant.

"In the first place, Dannie," said Uncle Juvinell, "for the benefit of the rest of the children, who are not so well informed upon such matters as yourself, we must see what a midshipman is. The lowest officer in the navy, but still several degrees removed from a common sailor, is a midshipman, who enters a man-of-war as a kind of pupil to study the art of navigation, and to acquaint himself with other matters connected with the seafaring life. A man-of-war, you must know, is the largest vessel, or ship of war, belonging to a nation; while all the ships fitted out at the public expense, together with the officers and seamen concerned in their keeping and management, make up what is called a navy. By navigation, we are to understand the art by which sailors are taught to conduct ships from one point to another. Now, a warrant is a writing that gives some one the right to do a thing or to enjoy it. Thus you see a midshipman's warrant would have given young Washington the right to go on board a man-of-war, where, as a kind of pupil, he would have learned the art of navigation, the management of ships, and many other things necessary to make a good sailor. The knowledge thus acquired, and the training to which he must needs have been subjected, would have fitted him in time to become an officer of the navy, such as a lieutenant or a captain, and, it may be, even an admiral."

"And what is an admiral?" inquired Willie.

"An admiral," replied Uncle Juvinell, "is the highest officer of the navy; he is to the armies of the sea what a general is to the armies of the land, and commands a squadron, or fleet, which, you must know, is a large number of armed ships, moving and acting in concert together."

"Does he fight with a sword?" inquired Bryce, who, it must be borne in mind, was the military young gentleman, who carried a wooden sword of his own.

"It is unusual," replied his uncle, "for either an admiral or a general to fight in person; it being their duty to put their armies in order of battle, and afterwards, during the fight, to control the movements of the different regiments or divisions by orders carried by aides to the officers under their command."

"You told us, uncle," said Willie, "that Washington received, along with the commission of adjutant-general, the rank of major. Now, what are we to understand by this?"

"A commission," replied his uncle, "is a writing, giving some one the right or authority to perform the duties of some office, and receive the pay and honors arising from the same. The duties of an adjutant-general you have already seen; and the commission received by young Washington to perform those duties made him equal in rank, not to a general, but to a major."

"I know you told us, uncle," said Ella, "what is meant by surveying; but I don't think that I clearly understand it yet."

"I will refer you to your brother Dannie," said Uncle Juvinell; "for he is looking very wise, as if somebody knew a thing or two, and could, were he but called upon, greatly enlighten somebody else. Out with it, Dannie, and let us have it."

"Surveying teaches the measurement of land," Dannie made haste to answer; "and a surveyor is one who measures land with the help of a long chain and compass and other instruments. Now, George Washington, for example" —

"That will do, Daniel," said his uncle, interrupting him: "you have made it as clear as daylight already; and I dare say your sister understands you perfectly, without the help of any example."

"Oh, I like to have forgotten one thing!" cried Willie. "Tell us what is meant by line of march, manœuvres on the battle-field, throwing up intrenchments, and the like."

To these points, Uncle Juvinell made answer: "An army, my nephew, is said to be on the line of march when it is moving from one place to another. A manœuvre is an evolution or a movement of an army, designed to mislead or deceive an enemy, or in some way to gain the advantage of him. An intrenchment is a breastwork or wall, with a trench or ditch running along the outside. The breastwork, being formed of the earth thrown up from the trench, serves as a protection against the shots of an enemy. The trench being quite as deep as the breastwork is high, renders it very difficult and dangerous for the works to be taken by storm; for the enemy must first descend into the ditch before he can reach and scale the wall, — an attempt always attended with the greatest peril to those who make it; for they who defend the works, fighting on top of the walls, have greatly the advantage of those beneath. Sometimes intrenchments run in straight or crooked lines, and sometimes enclose an irregular square or circle; and any piece of ground, or body of men, thus enclosed or fortified, is said to be intrenched."

"What a pity it is we can never know the name of the Lowland Beauty!" remarked Miss Laura regretfully; for she was getting to be quite old enough to be somewhat interested in matters of this kind.

"The name the young surveyor gave her," said Uncle Juvinell, "lends an interest to this part of his life, which a knowledge of her true name might never have awakened. Besides this, my dear niece, if you but be attentive to what I shall relate hereafter, you will learn many things touching the life and character of his mother Mary and his wife Martha far more worthy of your remembrance."

The clock struck ten; the fire burned low, and a heavy lid of ashes hid its great red eye. And now Uncle Juvinell bethought him that it must indeed be high bed-time for the little folks; and in conclusion he said, "Now, my dear children, I want you to bear well in mind what I have told you to-night, that you may be the better prepared for what I shall tell you to-morrow evening. And hereafter I would have you write down on your slates, while I go on with my story, whatever you may find difficult and shall wish to have more fully explained at the end of each evening's lesson. And now let us sing our evening hymn, and part for the night."

With that they joined their voices, as was their wont, in a sweet hymn of praise and thanks to the great Father of us all,—the little folks carrying the treble, while Uncle Juvinell managed the bass. This duly done, they came one by one, and kissed their dear old uncle a loving good-night; then crept to their happy beds to dream till morning of wooden-legged schoolmasters, little hatchets, wild rides on fiery untamed horses that were always sorrel, of life in the lonely wilderness, rambles without end up and down the mountains, and of skin-clad Indiana leaping and whirling in the war-dance.

IX.

INDIAN TROUBLES.

And now, said Uncle Juvinell, I see you are all agog, slate and pencil in hand, ready to jot down any question that may chance to pop into your busy young brains, to be asked and answered, for our further enlightenment, at the end of our evening lesson. So, without more ado, we will begin.

But, before trudging on further in our delightful journey, we must pause a moment, and turning square round, with our faces towards the long-ago years of the past, take a bird's-eye view of the early history of our country, that we may know exactly where we are when we come to find ourselves in the outskirts of that long and bloody struggle between the two great nations of England and France, commonly called the Seven Years' War, and sometimes the Old French War. Now, although this would not be as entertaining to your lively fancies as an Arabian tale or an Indian legend, yet you will by and by see very plainly that we could not have skipped it, without losing the sense of a great deal that follows; for it was during this war that our Washington first experienced the trials and hardships of a soldier's life, and displayed that courage, prudence, and ability, which in the end proved the salvation and glory of his native country.

In the first place, you must know, my dear children, that this beautiful land of ours, where now dwell the freest and happiest people the blessed sun ever shone upon, was, only a few hundred years ago, all a vast unbroken wilderness; a place where no one but savage Indians found a home, whose chief amusement was to fight and kill and scalp each other; and whose chief occupation was to hunt wild beasts and birds, upon whose flesh they fed, and with whose hairy skins and horns and claws and feathers they clothed and decked themselves. Where in the leafy summer-time may now be heard the merry plough-boy whistling "Yankee Doodle" over the waving corn, the wild Indian once wrestled with the surly bear, or met his ancient enemy in deadly fight. Nibbling sheep and grazing cattle now range the grassy hills and valleys where he was wont to give chase to the timid deer, or lie in wait for the monstrous buffalo. Huge steamers ply up and down our mighty rivers where he once paddled his little canoe. Splendid cities have risen, as if at the rubbing of Aladdin's enchanted lamp, where in the depths of the forest he once kindled the great council-fire, and met the neighboring tribes in the Big Talk. The very schoolhouse, where you little folks are now tripping so lightly along the flowery path of knowledge, may perhaps stand on the selfsame shady slope, where, of a long summer evening, he would sit at the door of his bark-built wigwam, smoking his long pipe, and watching his naked red children with a more fatherly smile than you can well imagine in one so fierce, as with many a hoop and yelp they played at "hide-and-seek" among the gray old trees and pawpaw thickets. On yonder hill-top, where we at this moment can see the windows of the house of God shining and glancing in the moonlight, he may have stood, with his face to the rising or setting sun, in mute worship before the Great Spirit.

But the stronger and wiser white man came; and, at his terrible approach, the red man, with all his wild remembrances, passed away, like an echo in the woods, or the shadow of an April cloud over the hills and valleys; and the place that once knew him shall know him no more for ever.

And yet it might have been far otherwise with him and with us, had not a certain Christopher Columbus chanced to light upon this Western World of ours, as he came hap-hazard across the wide Atlantic, where ship had never sailed before, in quest of a shorter passage to Asia.

By this great discovery, it was proved to the entire satisfaction of all who are in the least interested in the matter, that this earth upon which we live, instead of being long and flat, with sides and ends and corners like a great rough slab, was round, and hollow inside, like an India-rubber ball, and went rolling through empty space, round and round the sun, year after year, continually.

Of this bold and skilful sailor, the most renowned that ever lived, I should like to tell you many things; but, as we set out to give our chief attention to the story of Washington, we must deny ourselves this pleasure until the holidays of some merry Christmas yet to come, when your Uncle Juvinell, if he still keeps his memory fresh and green, will relate to you many wonderful things in the life of this great voyager, Columbus.

Up to this time, all the nations of Christendom had for ages upon ages been sunk in a lazy doze of ignorance and superstition. But, when tidings of the great discovery reached their drowsy ears, they were roused in a marvellous manner; and many of the richest and most powerful forthwith determined to secure, each to itself, a portion of the new-found region, by planting colonies; or, in other words, by making settlements therein.

For this purpose, they sent out fleets of ships across the Atlantic to these distant shores, laden with multitudes of men, who brought with them all manner of tools and implements wherewith to clear away the forests, till the soil, and build forts and cities, and arms to defend themselves against the attacks of the war-like savages. Thus, for example, Spain colonized Mexico; France, Canada; and England, that strip of the North-American continent, lying between the Alleghany Mountains and the Atlantic Ocean, now known as the eastern coast of the United States.

At first, the new-comers were received and treated with much kindness and hospitality by the natives: but it was not long before they discovered that they were likely to be robbed of their homes and hunting-grounds; when rage and jealousy took possession of their hearts, and from that time forward they never let slip an opportunity of doing all the mischief in their power to the hated intruders. Then began that long train of bloody wars between the two races, which have never ceased except with defeat or ruin of the weaker red man, and bringing him nearer and nearer to the day when he must either forsake his savage life, or cease to have an existence altogether.

Now, this may appear very unjust and wrong to my little friends; and, to some extent, it really was: but, in those days, might made right; or, in other words, the strong ruled the weak. And yet we are bound to believe that all this, in the long-run, has worked, and is still working, to the greatest good of the greatest number: for, had it been otherwise, all this beautiful land, now the home of a Christian and happy people, would have remained the dismal wilderness we have described it; answering no good end, as far as concerns the spread of truth and knowledge, and the cultivation of those useful arts which make a nation prosperous in peace, and strong in war.

Notwithstanding their troubles with the Indians, the hardships and privations to which the first settlers of a wild country are always exposed, and the shameful neglect with which they were treated by the mother-countries, the French and English colonies went on growing and thriving in a way that was wonderful to behold. At the end of a hundred and fifty years, or thereabouts, they had so grown in strength and increased in numbers, and had so widened their boundaries, that at last the continent, vast as it is, seemed too narrow to hold them both; and they began throwing up their elbows for more room, in a manner that would have been thought quite uncivil in a private individual at a dinner table or in a stage-coach.

Whereupon there arose a hot dispute between the kings of France and England as to whom belonged all that immense region stretching from the Alleghanies to the Mississippi, in the one direction; and, in the other, from the Ohio to the Great Lakes of the North.

The French claimed it by the right of discovery: by which they meant, that a certain Father Marquette had, nearly a hundred years before, discovered the Mississippi during his wanderings as a missionary among the Indians of the Far West. They pretended, that, as this pious man had paddled a little canoe up and down this splendid river a few hundred miles, his royal master, the King of France, was thereby entitled to all the lands watered by it, and the ten thousand streams that empty into it.

The English, on the other hand, claimed it by the right of purchase; having, as they said, bought it at a fair price of the Six Nations, a powerful league or union of several Indian tribes inhabiting the region round about the great lake's Erie and Ontario. What right the Six Nations had to it, is impossible to say. They claimed it, however, by the doubtful right of conquest; there being a tradition among them, that their ancestors, many generations before, had overrun the country, and subdued its inhabitants.

Now, the poor Indians who occupied the land in question were very indignant indeed when they heard that they and theirs had been sold to the white strangers by their red enemies, the Six Nations, whom they regarded as a flock of meddlesome crows, that were always dipping their ravenous bills into matters that did not in the least concern them; and their simple heads were sorely perplexed and puzzled, that two great kings, dwelling in far-distant countries, thousands of miles away beyond the mighty ocean, should, in the midst of uncounted riches, fall to wrangling with each other over a bit of wilderness land that neither of them had ever set eyes or foot on, and to which they had no more right than the Grand Caliph of Bagdad, or that terrible Tartar, Kublah Khan.

"Of all this land," said they, "there is not the black of a man's thumb-nail that the Six Nations can call their own. It is ours. More than a thousand moons before the pale-face came over the Big Water in his white-winged canoes, the Great Spirit gave it to our forefathers; and they handed it down, to be our inheritance as long as the old hills tell of their green graves. In its streams have we fished, in its woods have we hunted, in its sunny places have we built our wigwams, and in its dark and secret places have we fought and scalped and burnt our sworn enemies, without let or hinderance, time out of mind. Now, if the English claim all on this side of the Ohio, and the French claim all on this side of the Big Lakes, then what they claim is one and the same country,—the country whereon we dwell. Surely our white brothers must be dreaming. It is our hearts' desire, that our brothers, the English, keep on their side of the Ohio, and till the ground, and grow rich in corn; also that our brothers, the French, keep on their side of the lakes, and hunt in the woods, and grow rich in skins and furs. But you must both quit pressing upon us, lest our ribs be squeezed in and our breath be squeezed out, and we cease to have a place among men. We hold you both at arm's-length; and whoever pays good heed to the words we have spoken, by him will we stand, and with him make common cause against the other."

But to these just complaints of the poor Indian the French and English gave no more heed than if they who uttered them were so many whip-poor-wills crying in the woods. So they fell to wrangling in a more unreasonable manner than ever. Finally, to mend the matter (that is to say, make things worse), the French, coming up the Mississippi from the South, and down from the Great Lakes of the North, began erecting a chain of forts upon the disputed territory, to overawe the inhabitants thereof, and force the English to keep within the Alleghanies and the Atlantic. As a matter of course, the English regarded this as an insult to their dignity, and resolved to chastise the French for their impudence. And this it was that brought about that long and bloody struggle, the Old French War.

Thus, my dear children, do great and wise nations, professing to follow the humane teachings of the man-loving, God-fearing Jesus, often show no more truth and justice and honesty in their dealings with one another than if they were as ignorant of the Ten

The Farmer Boy and How He Became Commander-in-Chief

Commandments as the most benighted heathens, to whom even the name of Moses was never spoken. Yet, from your looks, I see that you are wondering within yourselves what all this rigmarole about England, France, the Six Nations, and disputed territories, can have to do with George Washington. Had you held a tight rein on your impatience a little while longer, you would have found out all about it, without the inconvenience of wondering; and hereafter, my little folks, rest assured that your Uncle Juvinell never ventures upon any thing without having all his eyes and wits about him, and that what he may tell you shall always prove instructive, although it may now and then—with no fault of his, however—seem to you somewhat dry and tedious.

X.

"BIG TALK" WITH "WHITE THUNDER."

But we are a little fast. In order to bring ourselves square again with our story, we must take one step backward, and begin afresh.

When tidings of these trespasses of the French reached the ears of Robert Dinwiddie, then Governor of Virginia, all his Scotch blood boiled within him, and he began forthwith casting in his mind what might be done to check or chastise such audacious proceedings.

Cooling down a little, however, he thought it would be better, before throwing his stones, to try what virtue might be found in grass. By which you are to understand, that he determined to write a letter to the French general, then stationed in a little fort near Lake Erie, inquiring by what authority these encroachments were made on the dominions of his royal master, the King of England; and demanding that they, the French, should abandon their forts, and withdraw their troops from the disputed territory, without delay, or else abide the consequences. He was well aware, that, to insure any thing like success in a mission so difficult and perilous, the person intrusted with it must needs be robust of body, stout of heart, clear of head; one inured to the hardships of a backwoods life, well acquainted with the habits and customs of the Indians, and withal a man of intelligence, polite address, and the strictest integrity of character. But one such man was to be found among ten thousand; and this was George Washington, who answered to the description in every particular, and was therefore chosen to perform this perilous undertaking, although he had not yet completed his twenty-second year.

Accordingly, having received from Governor Dinwiddie written instructions how to act when come into the enemy's country, Major Washington set out the next morning from Williamsburg, then the capital of Virginia, and made his way at once to Winchester, at that time a frontier settlement of the province, lying on the very edge of the wilderness. Here he spent several days in procuring supplies for the expedition, and raising a small party of hunters and pioneers to guard and bear him company. After some delay, he succeeded in procuring the services of seven men. Four of these were hardy backwoodsmen of experience, whose business it was to take care of the baggage and keep the party supplied with game. Mr. Davidson was to go along as Indian interpreter, and Mr. Gist as guide. A bolder and more enterprising pioneer than this Gist, by the by, was not to be found in all the Western wilds; and he is supposed by some historians to have been the first white man that ever brought down an elk or a buffalo in that paradise of hunters, green Kentucky. In addition to these, Washington took with him as French interpreter his old Dutch fencing-master, Capt. Van Braam. The worthy captain, however, seems to have been a far more expert master of sword-play than of the languages; for the jargon he was pleased to call an interpretation was often such a medley of half-learned English, half-remembered French, and half-forgotten Dutch, that they who listened would be nearly as much perplexed to see what he would be driving at, as if he were sputtering Cherokee into their ears.

All things being at last in readiness, the gallant little party, headed by our young Virginian, turned their faces towards the great Northwest; and, plunging into the wilderness, were soon beyond all traces of civilized man. The autumn was far advanced. The travelling was rendered toilsome, and even dangerous, by the heavy rains of this season, and early snows that had already fallen on the mountains, which had changed the little rills into rushing torrents, and the low bottom-lands into deep and miry swamps. Much delayed by these and the like hinderances, Washington, upon reaching the banks of the Monongahela, deemed it best to send two of the backwoodsmen with the baggage in canoes down this river to its mouth, where, uniting its waters with those of the Allegheny, it helped to form the great Ohio. Promising to meet them at this point, he and the rest of the party pushed thitherward by land on horseback. Reaching the Forks of the Ohio two days before the canoe-men, he spent the time in exploring the woods and hills and streams around, and was much struck with the advantages the place held out as a site for a military post. This, together with other items meriting attention that happened to him or occurred to his mind during the expedition, he carefully noted down in a journal which he kept, to be laid, in the

The Farmer Boy and How He Became Commander-in-Chief

form of a report, before Gov. Dinwiddie, upon his return. The following year, as a convincing proof to his countrymen how entirely they might rely on his foresight and judgment in such matters, French officers of skill and experience chose this very spot to be the site of Fort Duquesne, afterwards so famous in the border history of our country. Near the close of the war, this post fell into the hands of the English, who changed its name to that of Fort Pitt; which in time gave rise to the busy, thriving, noisy, dingy, fine young town of Pittsburg, a smoky-looking picture of which you may see any time you choose to consult your geography.

Instead of pushing on directly to the Lakes, Major Washington turned a little aside from his course, and went down the Ohio about twenty miles, to an Indian village called Logstown. Here, as had been previously arranged, he met a few sachems or chiefs of some of the Western tribes, to kindle a council-fire and have a Big Talk. He was received with much hospitality and courtesy by a stately old chief, whose Indian name you would not care to hear, as it would give Master Charlie's nut-crackers the jaw-ache to pronounce it. Among the English, however, as he was the head of a league or union of several tribes, he usually went by the name of the Half King. After the pipe had passed with all due gravity from mouth to mouth, and every warrior, chief, and white man present had taken a whiff or two, in sign that all was good-will and peace between them, Washington arose, and addressed the Half King in a short speech, somewhat after the following manner:—

"Your brother, the Governor of Virginia, has sent me with a letter to the big French captain, near Lake Erie. What is written therein deeply concerns you and your people as well as us. It was his desire, therefore, that you share with us the toils and dangers of this expedition, by sending some of your young men along with us, to guide us through the wilderness where there is no path, and be our safeguard against the wiles of cunning and evil-minded men we may chance to meet by the way. This he will look upon as a still further proof of the love and friendship you bear your brothers, the English. As a pledge of his faith in all this, and as a token of his love for his red brother, he sends this belt of wampum."

The Farmer Boy and How He Became Commander-in-Chief

Mr. Davidson having interpreted this speech, the Half King for some moments after sat smoking in profound silence, as if turning over in his mind what he had just heard, or as if waiting, according to Indian notions of etiquette on such occasions, to assure himself that the speaker had made an end of his say. He then arose, and spoke to the following effect:—

"I have heard the words of my young white brother, and they are true. I have heard the request of my brother the Governor of Virginia, and it is reasonable. At present, however, my young men are abroad in the forest, hunting game to provide against the wants of the coming winter, that our wives and children starve not when we are out upon the war-path. At the third setting of the sun from this time, they will be coming in; when I will not only send some of them with my young white brother, but will myself bear him company. For he must know that we have ceased to look upon the French as our friends. They have trespassed upon our soil; they have spoken words of insult and mockery to our oldest sachems. For this cause have my people resolved to return them the speech-belt they gave us at the Big Talk we had last winter at Montreal. It is that I may defy the big French captain to his teeth, and fling his speech-belt in his face, that I now go with my young brother, the Long Knife."

On the third day, as had been promised, the young men came in from hunting; from among whom the Half King chose eight or ten to serve as an additional escort to Major Washington during the expedition. Among these was a warrior of great distinction, who went by the tremendous name of White Thunder, and was keeper of the speech-belt. Now, you must know, that in Indian politics, when two tribes exchange speech-belts, it is understood to be an expression of peace and good-will between them; while to return or throw them away is the same as a declaration of war, or at least to be taken as a hint that all friendly intercourse between them is at an end. The "keeper of the speech-belt" was, therefore, a kind of "secretary of state" among these simple people.

Thus re-enforced by his red allies, Washington, who had grown somewhat impatient under this delay, gladly turned his face once more towards the Great Lakes. All this time, the rain had continued to fall with scarcely an hour's intermission. The streams and low meadow-lands were so flooded in consequence, that they were often obliged to wander many a weary mile over rugged highlands and through tangled forests, without finding themselves any nearer their journey's end. Now and then, coming to some muddy, swollen stream, in order to gain the opposite side without getting their baggage wet, they must needs cross over on rafts rudely constructed of logs and grape-vines, and make their horses swim along behind them. It was near the middle of December, before the little party, jaded and travel-stained, reached their destination.

Major Washington was received with true soldierly courtesy by the French general, to whom he at once delivered Gov. Dinwiddie's letter. A few days being requested for a due consideration of its contents, as well as the answer to be returned, he spent the time, as he had been instructed, in gaining all the information he could, without exciting suspicion, touching the designs of the French in the North-west,—to what extent they had won over the several Indian tribes to their interest; the number of troops they had brought into the territory; and the number, strength, and situation of the forts they had built. The fort where the French general then had his headquarters stood on the banks of a little river called French Creek, in which Washington observed lying, and bade his men count, a large number of canoes, to be used early in the following spring for transporting men and military stores down the Ohio. All the hints and items thus gathered he carefully noted down in his journal, to be laid, as I have told you already, in the form of a report, before Gov. Dinwiddie, upon his return.

Being wary and watchful, he was not long in discovering that the French were tampering with his Indian allies; tempting them, by the gayest of presents, the fairest of promises, and the hottest of firewater, to break faith with the English, and join their cause. These underhand dealings gave Washington much uneasiness of mind; and he complained to the French general, yet in a firm and dignified manner, of the unfair advantage thus taken of the besetting weakness of these poor people.

The Farmer Boy and How He Became Commander-in-Chief

Of course, the wily old Frenchman denied all knowledge of the matter; although we are bound to believe, that, as these tricks and intrigues were going on under his very nose, he must certainly have winked at, if he did not openly encourage them.

It is true that the Indians were by no means too nice to enrich themselves with French presents, and get drunk on French whiskey; yet, for all that, they turned a deaf ear to French promises, and, keeping their faith unbroken, remained as true as hickory to their friends the English. Even the Half King, stately and commanding as he was in council, yielded to the pleasing temptation along with the rest; and, for the greater part of the time, lay beastly drunk about the fort. When at last he came to his sober senses, he was not a little chopfallen upon being somewhat sternly reminded by Major Washington of the business that had brought him thither, the recollection of which he had seemingly drowned in his enemy's whiskey. Whereupon, as if to show that all his threats and promises had been made in good faith, he went forthwith to the French general, and delivered the grave oration he had composed for the occasion; at the same time returning the speech-belt White Thunder had brought, as a sign that all friendly relations between the French and his people were at an end.

At last, having received the answer to Gov. Dinwiddie's letter, and looked into matters and things about him as far as he could with prudence, Major Washington was now anxious to be away from the place where he had already been detained too long. During his stay, however, he had been treated with the greatest respect and courtesy by the accomplished Frenchman, who presented him, upon his departure, with a large canoe laden with a liberal supply of liquors and provisions, that lasted him and his men until they reached the Ohio.

To spare the horses as much as possible, Washington had sent them, with two or three of the men, by land to Venango, a fort about fifteen miles below; whither he now set out to follow them by water. The navigation of this little river, owing to its shallows and the masses of floating ice that here and there blocked up its channel, was difficult and toilsome in the extreme. Oftentimes, to prevent their frail canoes from being dashed to pieces against the rocks, would they be compelled to get out into the cold water for half an hour at a time, and guide them with their hands down the whirling and rapid current, and now and then even to carry them and their loads by land around some foaming cataract to the smoother water below. After an irksome little voyage, they reached Venango, fully satisfied that to go further by water was quite out of the question.

XI.

CHRISTMAS IN THE WILDERNESS.

Here, at Venango, Major Washington, much to his regret, was compelled to part company with the Half King and his other red allies. White Thunder, keeper of the speech-belt, had been so seriously injured in their passage down, as to be, for the present, quite unable to travel; and the rest would not think of leaving him, but needs must tarry there until their friend should be well enough to be brought in a canoe down the Alleghany.

Remounting their horses, our little party once more took their weary way through the wilderness. It was now the 22d of December. The weather was bitter cold; the snow fell thick and fast, and froze as it fell; and the bleak winds moaned drearily among the naked trees. The forest streams were frozen from bank to bank, yet often too thin to bear the weight of the horses; which rendered their crossing painful and hazardous indeed. To add to the discomfort of our travellers, the horses, from poor and scanty fare, had become too weak to be able longer to carry their allotted burdens. Moved with compassion at their pitiable plight, Washington dismounted from his fine saddle-horse, and loaded his with a part of the baggage; choosing rather to toil along on foot, than to take his ease at the expense of pain even to these poor brutes. His humane example was promptly followed by the rest of the party; and only the two men kept the saddle to whom was intrusted the care of the baggage.

You can well imagine, that a Christmas spent in this wild waste of leafless woods and snowy hills was any thing but a merry one to these poor fellows, so far away from their homes, which, at that moment, they knew to be so bright and cheerful with the mirth and laughter of "old men and babes, and loving friends, and youths, and maidens gay." And yet I dare say, that, even there, they greeted each other on that blessed morning with a brighter smile than usual, and called to their remembrance, that on that morn a babe was born, who, in the fulness of years, has grown to be the light and love and glory of the earth.

The Farmer Boy and How He Became Commander-in-Chief

Seeing that the half-famished beasts were growing weaker and weaker day by day, and that he would be too long in reaching his journey's end if he governed his speed by theirs, Washington left Capt. Van Braam in command of the party, and pushed forward with no other company than Mr. Gist. Armed with their trusty rifles, and clad in the light dress of the Indians, with no extra covering for the night but their watch-coats, and with no other baggage but a small portmanteau containing their food and Major Washington's important papers, they now made rapid headway, and soon left their friends far behind. The next day, they came upon an Indian village called Murdering Town; a name of evil omen, given it, perhaps, from its having been the scene of some bloody Indian massacre. What befell them here, I will tell you, as nearly as I can remember, in Mr. Gist's own words: —

"We rose early in the morning, and set out at seven o'clock, and got to Murdering Town, on the south-east fork of Beaver Creek. Here we met with an Indian whom I thought I had seen at Joncaire's, at Venango, when on our journey up to the French fort. This fellow called me by my Indian name, and pretended to be glad to see me. He asked us several questions; as, how we came to travel on foot, when we left Venango, where we parted with our horses, and when they would be there. Major Washington insisted on travelling by the nearest way to the forks of the Alleghany. We asked the Indian if he could go with us, and show us the nearest way. The Indian seemed very glad and ready to go with us; upon which we set out, and the Indian took the Major's pack. We travelled very brisk for eight or ten miles; when the Major's feet grew sore, and he very weary, and the Indian steered too much north-eastwardly. The Major desired to encamp; upon which the Indian asked to carry his gun, but he refused; and then the Indian grew churlish, and pressed us to keep on, telling us there were Ottawa Indians in those woods, and they would scalp us if we lay out; but go to his cabin, and we would be safe.

"I thought very ill of the fellow, but did not care to let the Major know I mistrusted him. But he soon mistrusted him as much as I did. The Indian said he could hear a gun from his cabin, and steered us northwardly. We grew uneasy, and then he said two whoops might be heard from his cabin. We went two miles further. Then the Major said he would stay at the next water, and we desired the Indian to stop at the next water; but, before we came to the water, we came to a clear meadow. It was very light, and snow was on the ground. The Indian made a stop, and turned about. The Major saw him point his gun towards us, and he fired. Said the Major,—

"'Are you shot?'

"'No,' said I.

"Upon which the Indian ran forward to a big standing white oak, and began loading his gun; but we were soon with him. I would have killed him; but the Major would not suffer me. We let him charge his gun. We found he put in a ball: then we took care of him. Either the Major or I always stood by the guns. We made him make a fire for us by a little run, as if we intended to sleep there. I said to the Major,—

"'As you will not have him killed, we must get him away, and then we must travel all night.'

"Upon which I said to the Indian,—

"'I suppose you were lost, and fired your gun?'

"He said he knew the way to his cabin: it was but a little distance.

"'Well,' said I, 'do you go home, and, as we are tired, we will follow your track in the morning; and here is a cake of bread for you, and you must give us meat in the morning.'

"He was glad to get away. I followed him, and listened until he was fairly out of the way; and then we went about half a mile, when we made a fire, set our compass, fixed our course, and travelled all night. In the morning, we were on the head of Piny Creek."

Thus you see, my dear children, from this adventure, upon what slight accidents sometimes hang the destinies, not only of individuals, but even of great nations; for had not this treacherous Indian missed his aim, and that too, in all likelihood, for the first time in a twelvemonth, it had never been our blessed privilege to know and love and reverence such a man as Washington; and that, instead of being the free-born, independent people that he made us, we might have been at this very moment throwing up our hats and wasting our precious breath in shouts of "Long life to Queen Victoria!"

All that day they walked on, weary and foot-sore, through the deep snow, without a trace of living man to enliven their solitary way. The cold gray of a winter's evening was deepening the shadows of the forest when they came to the banks of the Alleghany; and here a new disappointment awaited them. They had all along cheered themselves with the prospect of crossing this river on the ice: but they found it frozen for about fifty yards only from either bank; while the rest of the ice, broken into huge cakes, went floating swiftly down the main channel, crushing and grinding together, and filling the hollow woods around with doleful noises.

With heavy hearts they kindled their camp-fire, and cooked and ate their frugal supper; then, making themselves as comfortable as the piercing winds would allow, they lay down on their snowy beds to sleep, hopeful that the morrow would bring them better luck. Morning dawned, and yet brought with it no brighter prospect. Would you know what they did in this grievous state? Listen while I read Major Washington's own account of it, as we find it written in his journal:—

"There was no way for getting over but on a raft; which we set about, with but one poor hatchet, and finished just after sun-setting. This was a whole day's work. We next got it launched; then went on board of it, and set off. But, before we were half way over, we were jammed in the ice, in such a manner that we expected every moment our raft to sink, and ourselves to perish. I put out my setting-pole to try and stop the raft, that the ice might pass by; when the rapidity of the stream threw it with so much violence against the pole, that it jerked me out into ten feet of water: but I fortunately saved myself by catching hold of one of the raft-logs. Notwithstanding all our efforts, we could not get to either shore, but were obliged, as we were near an island, to quit our raft, and make to it. The cold was so extremely severe, that Mr. Gist had all his fingers, and some of his toes, frozen; and the water was shut up so hard, that we found no difficulty in getting off the island, on the ice, in the morning, and went to Mr. Frazier's."

Here, for a space, they stopped to rest and refresh themselves after the fatigue and exposure they had just undergone; and here, among other items of interest, they heard that Queen Aliquippa, an Indian princess, had been deeply offended that the young Long Knife had passed by her royal shanty, the month before, without calling to pay his compliments. Major Washington, well knowing that to humor their peculiar whims and fancies was the best mode of securing the good-will and friendship of these people, hastened at once to present himself before her copper majesty, and make what amends he could for his breach of etiquette. The present of a bottle of rum (over which, queen that she was, she smacked her lips), and of his old watch-coat, that would so handsomely set off her buckskin leggins, softened her ire completely, and made her, from that time forward, the stanch friend and ally of the English.

Travelling on a few miles further, they came to Mr. Gist's house, on the banks of the Monongahela, where Washington bought a horse to bear him to his journey's end, and parted with his trusty guide. He was now entirely alone; and a wide stretch of woods and mountains, swamps and frozen streams, still lay between him and the cheerful homes to whose comforts he had been so long a stranger. Now and then, the loneliness of the way would be for a moment enlivened by the sight of some sturdy backwoodsman, axe or rifle on shoulder, pushing westward, with his wife and children and dogs and household trumpery, to find a home in some still more distant part of the wilderness. It was midwinter, when, after having been absent eleven weeks on his perilous mission, our young Virginian, looking more like a wild Indian than the civil and Christian gentleman that he really was, rode into the town of Williamsburg, nor halted until he had alighted and hitched his horse in front of the governor's house.

XII.

WASHINGTON'S FIRST BATTLE.

Upon his arrival, Major Washington hastened at once to lay before Gov. Dinwiddie, and the Virginia Legislature then in session, the French general's letter, and the journal he had kept during the expedition.

In his letter, the French general spoke in high and flattering terms of the character and talents of young Washington; but, in language most decided and unmistakable, refused to withdraw his troops from the disputed territory, or cease building forts therein, as had been demanded of him, unless so ordered by his royal master, the King of France, to whose wishes only he owed respect and obedience. From the tenor of this letter, it was plainly enough to be seen (what might, in fact, have been seen before), that the French were not in the least inclined to give up, at the mere asking, all that they had been at so much pains and expense at gaining. It therefore followed, that as the title to this bit of forest land could not be written with the pen, on fair paper, in letters of Christian ink, it must needs be written with the sword, on the fair earth, in letters of Christian blood. By this, the little folks are to understand their Uncle Juvinell to mean that war alone could settle the question between them. And this unreasonable behavior, on the part of two great nations, has already, I doubt not, brought to your minds the story of two huge giants, who, chancing to meet one night, fell into a long and stormy dispute with each other about the possession of a fair bit of meadow-land they had happened to spy out at the same moment, where it lay in the lower horn of the moon; and who finally, like the silly monsters that they were, began belaboring each other with their heavy malls, as if the last hope of beating a little reason in were to beat a few brains out.

To drive and keep back the French and their Indian allies, Gov. Dinwiddie made a call on the Virginia militia, and wrote to the governors of some of the neighboring provinces, urging them, for their common defence, to do the same. To strengthen their borders, and give security to their frontier settlers, a small party of pioneers and carpenters were sent to build a fort at the Forks of the Ohio, as Washington had recommended in his journal. This journal, by the way, throwing, as it did, so much new light on the designs of the French in America, was thought worthy of publication, not only throughout the Colonies, but also in the mother-country. The good sense, skill, address, and courage shown by the young Virginian throughout the late expedition, had drawn upon him the eyes of his countrymen; and, from that time forward, he became the hope and promise of his native land. As a proof of this high regard, he was offered the command of the regiment to be raised: which, however, he refused to accept; for his modesty told him that he was too young and inexperienced to be intrusted with a matter of such moment to his country. To Col. Fry, an officer of some note in the province, the command of the regiment was therefore given; under whom he was quite willing to accept the post of lieutenant-colonel.

Notwithstanding the pressing danger that threatened all alike, the people were shamefully slow in answering the summons to arms. Washington had felt confident, that, at the very first tap of the drum, squads upon squads of active, sturdy, well-fed, well-clothed young farmers, moved by the same spirit with himself, would come flocking to his standard with their trusty rifles, powder-horns, and hunting-pouches, ready and eager to do their country service. Instead of this, however, there gathered, about him a rabble of ragamuffins and worthless fellows, who had spent their lives in tramping up and down the country, without settled homes or occupations.

Some were without hats and shoes; some had coats, and no shirts; some had shirts, and no coats; and all were without arms, or any keen desire to use them if they had them. All this disgusted and disheartened our youthful colonel not a little; for he was young, and had yet to learn that it is of just such stuff that the beginnings of armies are always made. The slender pay of a soldier was not enough to tempt the thriving yeomanry to leave their rich acres and snug firesides to undergo the hardships and dangers of a camp life; as if, by failing to answer their country's call, and fighting in its defence, they were not running a still greater risk of losing all they had.

To encourage the young men of the province to come forward, Gov. Dinwiddie caused it to be proclaimed, that two hundred thousand acres of the very best land on the head-waters of the Ohio should be divided between those that should enlist and serve during the war. This splendid offer had, in some small measure, the effect desired; so that, in a short time, something like an army was cobbled together, with which, poor and scantily provided as it was, they at last resolved to take the field.

Col. Washington, in command of the main body, was ordered to go on in advance, and cut a military road through the wilderness, in the direction of the new fort at the Forks of the Ohio, by way of the Monongahela; while Col. Fry was to remain behind with the rest of the troops, to bring up the cannon and heavy stores when the road should be opened. When the pioneers had cut their way about twenty miles beyond the frontier town of Winchester, there came a rumor, that the men who had been sent to build the fort at the Forks of the Ohio had all been surprised and captured by the French. In a few days, all doubts as to the truth of this report were set at rest by the men themselves, who came walking leisurely into camp, with their spades and axes on their shoulders, to every appearance quite well and comfortable.

For several days, they said, they had been working away on the fort quite merrily; when, early one morning, they were much surprised to see one thousand Frenchmen, in sixty bateaux, or boats, and three hundred canoes, with six pieces of cannon, dropping quietly down the Alleghany. The leader of this gallant little force summoned the fort to surrender in the short space of an hour, or else they would find their unfinished timber-work tumbling about their heads in a way that would not be altogether agreeable. No one with even half his wits about him would have for a moment thought of defending an unfinished fort with axes, spades, and augers, against a force of twenty times their number, backed by cannon and grape-shot. These men had all their wits about them, and, to prove it, gave up the fort without further parley; when the French captain marched in, and took formal possession of the wooden pen in the name of his most Christian majesty, the King of France; after which, with that gayety and good-humor so often to be observed among the French people, he invited the young ensign—who, in the absence of the captain, had been left in the command of the fort for that day—to dine and drink a glass of wine with him. He then suffered them all to depart in peace with his good wishes, and with their spades, carpenter's tools, and axes on their shoulders.

Col. Washington was deeply mortified at this intelligence; but, like the manly man that he was, he put a bright face on the matter, and, to keep up the spirits of his men, resolved to push on with the road with more vigor than ever. And a tremendous undertaking this was, I assure you. The tallest of trees were to be felled, the hugest of rocks to be split and removed, the deepest of swamps to be filled, and the swiftest of mountain torrents bridged over. With such hinderances, you will not wonder that they made but four miles a day. Now and then, the soldiers would be obliged to put their shoulders to the wheel, and help the poor half-famished horses with their heavy wagons up some rough and rocky steep. Thus over the gloomy mountains, and down the rugged defiles, and through a dark and lonely valley since called the Shades of Death, they forced their toilsome way. At last, after many weary days, they reached the banks of the Youghiogeny,—a romantic little river that went tumbling down the green hills in many a foaming waterfall; then, like a frolicsome school-boy nearing school, put on a demure and sober face, and quietly emptied itself into the more tranquil Monongahela. Here, to give his worn-out men and horses some repose after their severe and unceasing labors, Washington ordered a halt.

Being told by some friendly Indians that the baggage could be carried down this stream by water, he set out early one morning in a canoe, with four or five white men, and an Indian for a guide, to see for himself what truth there might be in this report. When they had rowed about ten miles, their Indian guide, after sulking for a little while, laid his oar across the canoe, and refused to go further. At first, this behavior appeared to them a little queer; but they were not long in discovering that it was only a way the cunning red rascal had of higgling to get more pay for his services. After some pretty sharp bargaining, Col. Washington promised to give him his old watch-coat and a ruffled shirt if he would go on; upon which, without more ado, he picked up his oar, and for the rest of the trip steered away blithely enough. You can well imagine what an uncommon swell this savage dandy, with his bare red legs, must have cut, a few days after, in his civilized finery, among the copper-cheeked belles of the woods. By the time they had rowed twenty miles further, Washington was satisfied, that, owing to the rocks and rapids, a passage down this river in the shallow canoes of the Indians was next to impossible.

Returning to camp, he soon afterwards received word from his old friend and ally, the Half King, that a party of French had been seen coming from the direction of Fort Duquesne, who were in all likelihood, by that time, somewhere in his close neighborhood. Upon hearing this, Washington deemed it prudent to fall back a few miles to the Great Meadows, a beautiful little plain, situated in the midst of woods and hills, and divided by a rivulet. Here he threw up strong intrenchments, cleared away the undergrowth, and prepared what he called "a charming field for an encounter." Shortly after, Mr. Gist, whom you well remember, came into camp, from his home on the Monongahela, with the tidings, that a party of French had been at his house on the day before, whom, from their appearance, he believed to be spies. Washington sent out some of his men on wagon-horses to beat the woods; who came in about dusk, without having, however, discovered any traces of the enemy. About nine o'clock that same night, an Indian runner came from the Half King with word, that some of his hunters had late that evening seen the tracks of two Frenchmen not five miles distant; and that, if Col. Washington would join him with some of his men, they would set out early in the morning in quest of the lurking foe.

Taking with him about forty men, and leaving the rest to guard the intrenchments, Washington set out forthwith for the Indian camp. Their way led them through tall and thick woods, that were then in the full leaf of early summer. As if to deepen their gloom, the sky was overcast with the blackest of clouds, from which the rain poured down in torrents; and the night, of course, was as dark as dark could be. No wonder, then, that they were continually losing their path, which was but a deer-track, and none of the plainest, even in broad daylight. When any one discovered that he had lost himself, he would shout, and set himself right again by the answering shouts of his comrades who might be so lucky as to be in the path at that moment. After blundering about all night through marshy thickets, slipping upon slimy rocks, and scrambling over the oozy trunks of fallen trees, they reached the Indian camp at daybreak in a somewhat moist and bedabbled plight, as you may well imagine. The Half King seemed overjoyed at seeing his young white brother once more; and, with true Indian hospitality, set before him and his men the best his camp afforded. After breakfasting heartily on bear's meat, venison, and parched corn, they all set out together, much refreshed, to seek what game might be in the wind. The Half King led the way to the spot where the two tracks had been seen the evening before; and, having found them, told two of his sharp-eyed hunters to follow the trail until they could bring some tidings of the feet that had made them. Like hounds on the scent of a fox, they started off at a long trot; only pausing now and then to look more closely at the leaves, to make sure they were right, and not on a cold scent. In a short time, they came back with word that they had spied twenty-five or thirty French and Canadians encamped in a low, narrow bottom, between high and steep hills, who looked as if they were desirous of concealment. Whereupon Washington proposed that the two parties should divide, and, stealing upon the enemy from opposite directions, surprise and capture him, if possible, without the shedding of blood. To this the Half King agreed; and, parting, they moved off in profound silence, each on their separate way.

A sudden turn of the hollow, down which they had been making their way for several minutes, brought Washington and his party, ere they were well aware, in full view of the enemy. Some were cooking their morning's meal, some were preparing their arms for the day's excursion, some were lounging, and all were merry. But, seeing as soon as seen, they ran with all speed to their guns, that were leaned against the trees hard by, and, without more ado, began firing in so brisk and earnest a manner, that left the Virginians no choice but to return it, which they did with spirit. About the same time, the Half King and his warriors came down to the bottom of the hill on the opposite side of the hollow, and, screening themselves behind a bit of rising ground, joined the music of their rifles with the rest. For about fifteen minutes, the skirmish was kept up with great spirit on both sides; when the French, having lost ten of their number (among whom was their leader, Capt. de Jumonville), surrendered, and yielded up their arms. Washington had one man shot dead at his side, and three men wounded; but his Indian allies, protected as they were by the rising ground, came off without the loss of a single feather or porcupine-quill. Unluckily, in the heat of the encounter, a swift-footed Canadian, better, no doubt, at dodging than shooting, managed to make his escape, and carried the news to Fort Duquesne.

The Half King and his warriors, I am sorry to tell you, would have butchered the prisoners in cold blood, had not Washington sternly forbidden them. They therefore consoled themselves as best they might for this disappointment by scalping the dead; which, however, yielded them but sorry comfort, as there were but ten scalps to be divided among forty warriors.

The Half King was much offended by this humane interference, on the part of his young white brother, in behalf of the prisoners; for he seemed to think, that as they were spies, and French spies at that, they richly deserved to be scalped alive. Such milk-and-water, half-way measures might do for pale-faces, but were not the sort of entertainment to be relished by a genuine Indian brave of the first water, or, to speak more to the point, of the first blood.

Without, however, in the least heeding these muttered grumblings of the worthy old chief, who had his failings along with the rest of mankind, Col. Washington took the prisoners to his camp, where he treated them with even more kindness and courtesy than they as spies deserved. From thence he sent them under a strong guard to Williamsburg, and wrote to Gov. Dinwiddie, begging him to treat them with all the humanity due to prisoners of war, but to keep a strict watch over them, as there were among them two or three very cunning and dangerous men.

This encounter, commonly called the Jumonville affair, caused a great sensation, not only throughout the Colonies, but also in France and England; for it was there, as you must know, in that remote and obscure little valley, that flowed the first blood of this long and eventful war. It was Washington's first battle; and, being a successful one, much inspirited him. In a letter written at this time to his brother Augustine, after touching upon the particulars of this skirmish, he says, "I heard the bullets whistle; and, believe me, there is something charming in the sound."

XIII.

FORT NECESSITY.

About this time, Col. Fry died at Wills's Creek, where he had lain ill of a fever for several weeks; and Washington, as the next in rank, was obliged to take command of the regiment. Although this change brought with it an increase of pay and honors, yet it caused him the sincerest regret; for even then, young as he was, he had the good of his country more earnestly at heart than his own private advantage. He said, and with unfeigned modesty, that he feared he was scarcely equal to the discharge of such high and responsible duties, without the aid and counsel of some older and more experienced officer.

Capt. de Villiers was now commander of the French at Fort Duquesne. When tidings of the late encounter reached this officer through the swift-footed Canadian, he swore a deep oath that he would chastise the audacious young Virginian for what he chose to call this barbarous outrage, and avenge the death of De Jumonville, whose brother-in-law, as ill luck would have it, he chanced to be. Foreseeing his danger, and to defend himself against the superior force he knew would be brought against him, Col. Washington set about forthwith to strengthen his works. He dug the ditches deeper, raised the breastworks higher, and surrounded the whole with a row of palisades, firmly planted in the ground, and set so close together as scarcely to allow of a gun-barrel passing between them.

Owing to the shameful neglect of those whose duty it was to send up supplies, he and his men suffered much from the want of food,— many days at a stretch sometimes passing by without their tasting bread. To aggravate this new distress, the Half King and many of his warriors, with their wives and children, now sought refuge in the fort from the vengeance of the French and their savage allies; which added nothing to their strength, and only increased the number of hungry mouths to be fed. To this place, then, where gaunt famine pinched them from within and watchful enemies beset them from without, Washington gave the fitting name of Fort Necessity. Luckily for them, while in this pitiable plight, days and days passed by, and still no avenging De Villiers showed himself, though alarms were frequent.

Col. Washington now ordered Major Muse to bring up the rest of the troops that had been waiting all this while at Wills's Creek, with the heavy stores and cannon. To reward the friendly Indians for their services and fidelity, Major Muse brought with him presents of hatchets and knives, guns, powder and lead, tin cups, needles and pins, beads, and dry-goods of every gaudy hue, and it may be, although we can only guess it, a ruffled shirt or two. In addition to these, there came a number of silver medals for the chief sachems, sent by Gov. Dinwiddie at the suggestion of Col. Washington, who well knew how much these simple people prize little compliments of this kind. Major Muse handed out the presents, while Washington hung the medals about the necks of the sachems, which yielded them far more delight, you will be sorry to hear, than their good old missionary's catechism. This was done with all that show and parade so dear to an Indian's heart; and, to give a still finer edge to the present occasion, they christened each other all over again: that is to say, the red men gave the white men Indian names, and the white men gave the red men English names. Thus, for example, Washington gave the Half King the name of Dinwiddie, which pleased him greatly; while he, in his turn, bestowed on his young white brother a long, high-sounding Indian name, that you could pronounce as readily spelt backwards as forwards. Fairfax was the name given a young sachem, the son of Queen Aliquippa, whose eternal friendship to the English, it must be borne in mind, had been secured by Washington, the previous winter, by the present of an old coat and a bottle of rum.

By the advice of his old and much-esteemed friend, Col. William Fairfax, Washington had divine worship in the fort daily, in which he led; and, thanks to the early teachings of his pious mother, he could do this, and sin not. Solemn indeed, my dear children, and beautiful to behold, must have been that picture,—that little fort, so far away in the heart of the lonely wilderness, with its motley throng of painted Indians and leather-clad backwoodsmen gathered round their young commander, as, morning and evening, he kneeled in prayer before the Giver of all good, beseeching aid and protection, and giving thanks.

As if to put his manhood and patience to a still severer test, there came to the fort about this time an independent company of one hundred North Carolinians, headed by one Capt. Mackay, who refused to serve under him as his superior officer. As his reason for this conduct, Mackay argued that he held a royal commission (that is to say, had been made a captain by the King of England), which made him equal in rank, if not superior, to Washington, who held only a provincial commission, or had been made a colonel by the Governor of Virginia. This, in part, was but too true; and it had been a source of dissatisfaction to Washington, that the rank and services of colonial officers should be held at a cheaper rate than the same were valued at in the royal army. It wounded his honest, manly pride, and offended his high sense of justice; and he had already resolved in his own mind to quit such inglorious service, as soon as he could do so without injury to the present campaign, or loss of honor to himself. To most men, the lofty airs and pretensions of Capt. Mackay and his Independents would have been unbearable; but he kept his temper unruffled, and, with a prudence beyond his years, forbore to do or say any thing that would lead to an angry outbreak between them; and as they chose to encamp outside the fort, and have separate guards, he deemed it wisest not to trouble himself about them, only so far as might concern their common safety.

Days, and even weeks, had now passed away, and still no enemy had come to offer him battle. His men were becoming restless from inaction; and the example of the troublesome Independents had already begun to stir up discontent among them, which threatened, if not checked in season, to end in downright insubordination. As the surest remedy for these evils, Washington resolved to push forward with the road in the direction of Fort Duquesne, and carry the war into the enemy's own country. Requesting Capt. Mackay to guard the fort during his absence, he set out with his entire force of three hundred men, and again began the toilsome work of cutting a road through the wilderness. The difficulties they had now to overcome were even greater than those which beset them at the outset of their pioneering. The mountains were higher, the swamps deeper, the rocks more massive, the trees taller and more numerous, the torrents more rapid, the days more hot and sultry, and the men and horses more enfeebled by poor and scanty food. You will not wonder, then, that they were nearly two weeks in reaching Mr. Gist's plantation on the Monongahela, a distance of but fifteen miles.

But hardly had they pitched their tents, and thrown themselves on the grass to snatch a little rest, when there came the disheartening intelligence, brought in by their Indian spies, that Capt. de Villiers had been seen to sally from Fort Duquesne but a few hours before, at the head of a force of five hundred French and four hundred Indians, and must by that time be within a few miles of the Virginia camp. For three hundred weary and hungry men to wait and give battle to a force three times their number, fresh and well fed, was a thing too absurd to be thought of for a single moment. Washington, therefore, as their only chance of safety, ordered a hasty retreat, hoping that they might be able to reach the settlements on Wills's Creek before the enemy could overtake him. The retreat, however, was any thing but a hasty one; for the poor half-famished horses were at last no longer able to drag the heavy cannon and carry the heavy baggage. Moved with pity for the lean and tottering beasts, Washington dismounted from his fine charger, and gave him for a pack-horse; which humane example was promptly followed by his officers. Yet even this was not enough: so, while some of the jaded men loaded their backs with the baggage, the rest, as jaded, dragged the artillery along the stony roads with ropes, rather than that it should be left behind to fall into the hands of the enemy. For this good service, rendered so willingly in that hour of sore distress, they went not unrewarded by their generous young commander.

Capt. Mackay and his company of Independents had, at Washington's request, come up a little while before, and now joined in the retreat. But they joined in nothing else; for, pluming themselves upon their greater respectability as soldiers of his Britannic majesty, they lent not a helping hand in this hour of pressing need, although the danger that lurked behind threatened all alike. They marched along, these coxcombs, daintily picking their way over the smoothest roads, and too genteel to be burdened with any thing but their clean muskets and tidy knapsacks. This ill-timed and insolent behavior served only to aggravate the trials of the other poor fellows all the more; and when, at last, they had managed to drag the cannon and the wagons and themselves to Fort Necessity, they were so overcome with fatigue and hunger, and so moved with indignation at the conduct of the Independents, that they threw down their ropes and packs, and flatly refused to be marched further. Seeing their pitiful plight, and that it would be impossible to reach the settlements, Col. Washington, as their last chance of safety, turned aside, and once more took shelter in his little fort.

As Capt. Mackay and his company of gentlemen fighters had done nothing towards strengthening the works during his absence, Washington ordered a few trees to be felled in the woods hard by, as a still further barrier to the approach of the enemy. Just as the last tree went crashing down, the French and their Indian allies, nine hundred strong, came in sight, and opened a scattering fire upon the fort, but from so great a distance as made it little more than an idle waste of powder and lead. Suspecting this to be but a feint of the crafty foe to decoy them into an ambuscade, Washington ordered his men to keep within the shelter of the fort, there to lie close, and only to shoot when they could plainly see where their bullets were to be sent.

A light skirmishing was kept up all day, and until a late hour in the night; the Indians keeping the while within the shelter of the woods, which at no point came within sixty yards of the palisades. Whenever an Indian scalp-lock or a French cap showed itself from among the trees or bushes, it that instant became the mark of a dozen sharpshooters watching at the rifle-holes of the fort. All that day, and all the night too, the rain poured down from one black cloud, as only a summer ruin can pour, till the ditches were filled with water, and the breastworks nothing but a bank of miry clay; till the men were drenched to the skin, and the guns of many so dampened as to be unfit for use.

About nine o'clock that night, the firing ceased; and shortly after a voice was heard, a little distance beyond the palisades, calling upon the garrison, in the name of Capt. de Villiers, to surrender.

The Farmer Boy and How He Became Commander-in-Chief

Suspecting this to be but a pretext for getting a spy into the fort, Col. Washington refused to admit the bearer of the summons. Capt. de Villiers then requested that an officer be sent to his quarters to parley; giving his word of honor that no mischief should befall him, or unfair advantage be taken of it. Whereupon, Capt. Van Braam, the old Dutch fencing-master, being the only French interpreter conveniently at hand, was employed to go and bring in the terms of surrender. He soon came back; but the terms were too dishonorable for any true soldier to think of accepting. He was sent again, but with no better result. The third time, Capt. de Villiers sent written articles of capitulation; which, being in his own language, must needs be first translated before an answer could be returned. By the flickering light of one poor candle, which could hardly be kept burning for the pouring rain, the Dutch captain read the terms he had brought, while the rest stood round him, gathering what sense they could from the confused jumbling of bad French, and worse English he was pleased to call a translation. After this, there followed a little more parleying between the hostile leaders; when it was at last settled that the prisoners taken in the Jumonville affair should be set at liberty; that the English should build no forts upon the disputed territories within a twelvemonth to come; and that the garrison, after destroying the artillery and military stores, should be allowed to march out with all the honors of war, and pursue their way to the settlements, unmolested either by the French or their Indian allies. When we take into account the more than double strength of the enemy, the starving condition of the garrison (still further weakened as it was by the loss of twelve men killed and forty-three wounded), and the slender hope of speedy succor from the settlements, these terms must be regarded as highly honorable to Col. Washington; and still more so when we add to this the fact, that the Half King and his other Indian allies had deserted him at the first approach of danger, under the pretext of finding some safer retreat for their wives and children. Whether they failed from choice, or hinderance to return, and take part in the action, can never now be known with certainty.

Thus the dreary night wore away; and, when the dreary morning dawned, they destroyed the artillery and the military stores, preparatory to their setting forth on their retreat. As all the horses had been killed or lost the day before, they had no means of removing their heavy baggage: they therefore secured it as best they might, hoping to be able to send back for it from the settlements. Still in possession of their small-arms, they then marched out of the fort with all the honors of war,—fifes playing, drums beating, and colors flying. They had gone but a few yards from the fort, when a large body of Indians pounced with plundering hands upon the baggage. Seeing that the French could not or would not keep them back, Washington, to disappoint them of their booty, ordered his men to set fire to it, and destroy all they could not bring away upon their backs.

This done, they once more took up their line of march; and a melancholy march it was. Between them and the nearest settlements, there lay seventy miles of steep and rugged mountain-roads, over which they must drag their weary and aching limbs before they could hope to find a little rest. Washington did all that a kind and thoughtful commander could to keep up the flagging spirits of his men; sharing with them their every toil and privation, and all the while maintaining a firm and cheerful demeanor. Reaching Wills's Creek, he there left them to enjoy the full abundance which they found awaiting them at that place; and, in company with Capt. Mackay, repaired at once to Williamsburg to report the result of the campaign to Gov. Dinwiddie.

A short time after, the terms of surrender were laid before the Virginia House of Burgesses, and received the entire approval of that wise body; who, although the expedition had ended in defeat and failure, most cheerfully gave Col. Washington and his men a vote of thanks, in testimony of their having done their whole duty as good and brave and faithful soldiers.

XIV.

GENERAL BRADDOCK.

Having brought the campaign to an honorable if not successful end, Col. Washington threw up his commission, and left the service. This had been his determination for some time past; and he felt that he could do so now without laying his conduct open to censure or suspicion, having within his own breast the happy assurance, that, in the discharge of his late trust, he had acted the part of a faithful soldier and true patriot, seeking only his country's good. The reasons that led him to take this step need not be repeated, as you will readily understand them, if you still bear in mind what I told you a short time since touching those questions of rank which caused the difficulty between him and Capt. Mackay.

A visit to his much-beloved mother was the first use he made of his leisure. The profound love and reverence that never failed to mark his conduct towards his mother were among the most beautiful traits of his character. The management of the family estate, and the education of the younger children, were concerns in which he ever took the liveliest interest; and to make these labors light and easy to her by his aid or counsel was a pleasure to him indeed. This grateful duty duly done, he once more sought the shelter of Mount Vernon, to whose comforts he had been for so many months a stranger. The toils of a soldier's life were now exchanged for the peaceful labors of a husbandman. Nor did this change, to his well-ordered mind, bring with it any idle regrets; for the quiet pursuits of a farmer's life yielded him, young, ardent, and adventurous as he was, scarcely less delight than the profession of arms, and even more as he grew in years.

The affair of the Great Meadows roused the mother-country at last to a full sense of the danger that threatened her possessions in America. Accordingly, to regain what had been lost, money, and munitions of war, and a gallant little army fitted out in the completest style of that day, were sent over with all possible expedition, under the command of Major-Gen. Braddock.

The Farmer Boy and How He Became Commander-in-Chief

From the shrubby heights of Mount Vernon, Washington could look down, and behold the British ships-of-war as they moved slowly up the majestic Potomac, their decks thronged with officers and soldiers dressed in showy uniform, their polished arms and accoutrements flashing back the cold, clear light of the February sun. From their encampment at Alexandria, a few miles distant, he could hear the booming of their morning and evening guns, as it came roiling over the hills and through the woods, and shook his quiet home like a sullen summons to arms. Often, no longer able to keep down his youthful ardor, he would mount his horse, and, galloping up to the town, spend hours there in watching the different companies, as with the precision of clockwork they went through their varied and difficult evolutions. At these sights and sounds, all the martial spirit within him took fire again.

To Gen. Braddock, who commanded all the forces in America, provincial as well as royal, Gov. Dinwiddie and other Virginia notables spoke in the highest terms of the character of young Washington; giving him at the same time still further particulars of the brave and soldierly conduct he had so signally shown during the campaign of the previous year. They took pleasure, they said, in recommending him as one whose skill and experience in Indian warfare, and thorough acquaintance with the wild country beyond the borders, were such as could be turned to the greatest advantage in the course of the following campaign.

Desirous of securing services of such peculiar value, Braddock sent our young Virginian a courteous invitation to join his staff; offering him the post of volunteer aide-de-camp, with the rank of colonel. Here was an opportunity of gratifying his taste for arms under one of the first generals of the day. Could he do it without the sacrifice of honor or self-respect? Although he had left the service for the best of reasons, as you must bear in mind, yet there was nothing in these reasons to hinder him from serving his country, not for pay, but as a generous volunteer, bearing his own expenses. Besides, such a post as this would place him altogether above the authority of any equal or inferior officer who might chance to hold a king's commission. Debating thus with himself, and urged on by his friends, he accepted

The Farmer Boy and How He Became Commander-in-Chief

Braddock's invitation, and joined his staff as volunteer aide-de-camp.

Now, would you know what an aide-de-camp is? Wait, and you will find out for yourselves when we come to the battle of the Monongahela, where Braddock suffered his gallant little army to be cut to pieces by the French and Indians.

When Mrs. Washington heard that her son was on the eve of joining the new army, full of a mother's fears, she hastened to entreat him not again to expose himself to the dangers and trials of a soldier's life. Although the army was the only opening to distinction at that time in the Colonies, yet, to have him ever near her, she would rather have seen him quietly settled at his beautiful homestead, as an unpretending farmer, than on the high road to every worldly honor at the risk of life or virtue. Ever mindful of her slightest wishes, her son listened respectfully to all her objections, and said all he could to quiet her motherly fears: but, feeling that he owed his highest duty to his country, he was not to be turned from his steadfast purpose; and, taking an affectionate leave of her, he set out to join his general at Fort Cumberland.

Fort Cumberland was situated on Wills's Creek, and had just been built by Braddock as a gathering point for the border; and thither he had removed his whole army, with all his stores, and munitions of war. Upon further acquaintance, Washington found this old veteran a man of courteous though somewhat haughty manners, of a hasty and uneven temper, strict and rigid in the discipline of his soldiers, much given to martial pomp and parade, and self-conceited and wilful to a degree that was sometimes scarcely bearable. He was, however, of a sociable and hospitable turn; often inviting his officers to dine with him, and entertaining them like princes. So keen a relish had he for the good things of the table, that he never travelled without his two cooks, who were said to have been so uncommonly skilful in their line of business, that they could take a pair of boots, and boil them down into a very respectable dish of soup, give them only the seasoning to finish it off with. The little folks, however, must be very cautious how they receive this story, as their Uncle Juvinell will not undertake to vouch for the truth of it.

The Farmer Boy and How He Became Commander-in-Chief

The contractors—that is to say, the men who had been engaged to furnish the army with a certain number of horses, pack-saddles, and wagons, by a certain time, and for a certain consideration—had failed to be as good as their word, and had thereby seriously hindered the progress of the campaign. As might have been expected, this was enough to throw such a man as Braddock into a towering passion; and, to mend his humor, the governors of the different provinces were not as ready and brisk to answer his call for men and supplies as he thought he had a right to expect.

So he poured forth his vials of wrath upon whomsoever or whatsoever chanced to come uppermost. He stormed at the contractors; he railed at the governors, and sneered at the troops they sent him; he abused the country in general, and scolded about the bad roads in particular.

Washington, with his usual clearness of insight into character, soon saw, to his deep disappointment, that this was hardly the man to conduct a wilderness campaign to any thing like a successful end, however brave the testy old veteran might be, and expert in the management of well-drilled regulars in the open and cultivated regions of the Old World. Of the same opinion was Dr. Franklin, who, being at that time Postmaster-General of all the Colonies, came to Braddock's quarters at Fort Cumberland to make some arrangements for transporting the mail to and from the army during the progress of the expedition. I will read you his own lively account of this interview, as it will enable you to see more clearly those faults of Braddock's character that so soon after brought ruin on his own head, and disgrace upon English arms in America.

"In conversation with him one day, he was giving me some account of his intended progress. 'After taking Fort Duquesne,' said he, 'I am to proceed to Niagara; and, having taken that, to Frontenac, if the season will allow; and I suppose it will, for Duquesne can hardly detain me above three or four days: and then I can see nothing that can obstruct my march to Niagara.'

"Having before revolved in my mind the long line his army must make in their march by a very narrow road to be cut for them through the woods and bushes, and also what I had heard of a former defeat of fifteen hundred French who invaded the Illinois country, I had conceived some doubts and some fears for the event of the campaign; but I ventured only to say, 'To be sure, sir, if you arrive well before Duquesne with these fine troops, so well provided with artillery, the fort, though completely fortified and assisted with a very strong garrison, can probably make but a short resistance. The only danger I apprehend of obstruction to your march is from the ambuscades of the Indians, who, by constant practice, are dexterous in laying and executing them; and the slender line, nearly four miles long, which your army must make, may expose it to be attacked by surprise on its flanks, and to be cut like thread into several pieces, which, from their distance, cannot come up in time to support one another.' He smiled at my ignorance, and replied,"'These savages may, indeed, be a formidable enemy to raw American militia; but upon the king's regular and disciplined troops, sir, it is impossible they should make an impression.'

"I was conscious of an impropriety in my disputing with a military man in matters of his profession, and said no more."

In the course of this interview, Franklin chanced to express a regret that the army had not been landed in Pennsylvania, where, as every farmer kept his own wagon and horses, better means would have been more readily found for transporting the troops, with their heavy guns and munitions of war, across the country and over the mountains. Quick to take a hint, Braddock made haste to request him, as a man of standing in his colony, to furnish him, in the king's name, one hundred and fifty wagons, and four horses to each wagon, besides a large number of pack-horses and pack-saddles. This, Franklin readily undertook to do; and went about it with such diligence, that by the latter part of spring, even before the time set, he had fulfilled his promise to the last letter; and Braddock had now the satisfaction of seeing his army, after all these vexatious delays, in a condition to move forward.

Meanwhile, Washington was all attention to affairs in camp, and was daily gaining fresh insight into the art of war, as understood and practised in the most civilized countries of the Old World. Every day the men were drilled, and passed under review; their arms and accoutrements carefully inspected by their officers, to make sure that they were in perfect order, and ready for use at a moment's notice. Sentinels and guards were stationed in and about the camp, day and night.

So strict was the watch kept by this lynx-eyed old general over the morals of his men, that drunkenness was punished with severe confinement; and any one found guilty of theft was drummed out of his regiment, after receiving five hundred stripes on his bare back. Every Sunday, the soldiers were called together, under the colors of their separate regiments, to hear divine service performed by their chaplains.

To lend variety to the scene, the Indians of the neighboring wilderness came flocking in to join their fortunes with the English, or bring information of the movements or designs of the French. Among these came his old friend and ally, White Thunder, keeper of the speech-belt; and Silver Heels, a renowned warrior, so called, no doubt, from his being uncommonly nimble of foot. Also, as we shall meet him again hereafter, should be mentioned another sachem, whose Indian name the little folks must excuse their Uncle Juvinell from giving them in full. By your leave, then, for the sake of brevity and convenience, we will call him by the last two syllables of his name, Yadi. From them Washington learned, much to his regret, that his red brother, the Half King, had died a few months before; having, as the conjurors or medicine-men of his tribe pretended, been bewitched by the French for the terrible blow he had dealt them at the battle of Jumonville, which had filled them with such terror, that they dared not hope for safety in the wide earth till certain that he walked and ate and slept no more among living men.

Although Braddock held these savage allies in high contempt, yet when Washington pointed out to him how much was to be gained by their friendship, and how much to be lost by their enmity, he was persuaded, for that one time at least, to treat them with marked respect and distinction.

To give them an overwhelming idea of the power and splendor of English arms, he received them with all the honors of war,—fifes playing, drums beating, and the regulars lowering their muskets as they passed on to the general's tent. Here Braddock received them in the midst of his officers, and made them a speech of welcome, in the course of which he told them of the deep sorrow felt by their great father, the King of England, for the death of his red brother, the Half King; and that, to console his red children in America for so grievous a loss, as well as to reward them for their friendship and services to the English, he had sent them many rich and handsome presents, which they should receive before leaving the fort. This speech was answered by a dozen warriors in as many orations, which being very long and very flowery, and very little to the point, bored their English listeners dreadfully. The peace-pipe smoked and the Big Talk ended, Braddock, by way of putting a cap on the grand occasion, ordered all the fifes to play, and drums to beat, and, in the midst of the music, all the guns in the fort to be fired at once. He then caused a bullock to be killed, and roasted whole, for the refreshment of his Indian guests.

The Indians, in their turn, to show how sensible they were of the honor done them by this distinguished reception, entertained the English by dancing their war-dances and singing their war-songs: by which you are to understand that they jumped and whirled and capered about in a thousand outlandish antics till they grew limber and weak in the knees, and yelped and bellowed and howled till their bodies were almost empty of breath; when, from very exhaustion, they hushed their barbarous din, and night and slumber fell on the camp. In the daytime, these lords of the forest, tricked out in all their savage finery, their faces streaked with war-paint and their scalp-locks brave with gay bunches of feathers, would stalk about the fort, big with wonder over every thing they saw. Now and then, they would follow with admiring eyes the rapid and skilful movement of the red-coated regulars, as one or other of the regiments, like some huge machine, went through their martial exercises; or, standing on the ramparts, they would watch with still keener zest and interest the young officers as they amused themselves by racing their horses outside the fort.

As ill luck would have it, these warriors had brought with them their wives and children, among whom were many very pretty Indian girls, with plump, round forms, little hands and feet, and beady, roguish eyes. As female society was not by any means one of the charms of life at Fort Cumberland, the coming of these wild beauties was hailed with the liveliest delight by the young English officers, who, the moment they laid eyes on them, fell to loving them to desperation. First among these forest belles was one who went by the expressive name of Bright Lightning; so called, no doubt, from being the favorite daughter of White Thunder. It being noised abroad that she was a savage princess of the very first blood, she, of course, at once became the centre of fashionable attraction, and the leading toast of all the young blades in camp. No sooner, however, did the warriors get wind of these gallantries, than they were quite beside themselves with rage and jealousy, and straightway put an end to them; making the erring fair ones pack off home, bag and baggage, sorely to their disappointment, as well as to that of the young British lions, who were quite inconsolable for their loss.

This scandalous behavior on the part of the English—of which, however, your Uncle Juvinell may have spoken more lightly than he ought—was, as you may well believe, very disgusting to Washington, who was a young man of the purest thoughts and habits. As may be naturally supposed, it gave deep and lasting offence to the sachems; and when to this is coupled the fact, that their wishes and opinions touching war-matters were never heeded or consulted, we cannot wonder that they one by one forsook the English, with all their warriors, and came no more.

Foreseeing this, and well knowing what valuable service these people could render as scouts and spies, Washington had gone to Braddock, time and again, warning him to treat them with more regard to their peculiar whims and customs, if he did not wish to lose the advantages to be expected from their friendship, or bring upon him the terrible consequences of their enmity. As this wise and timely advice came from a young provincial colonel, the wrong-headed old general treated it, of course, with high disdain, and to the last remained obstinate in the belief that he could march to the very heart of the continent without meeting an enemy who could withstand his well-drilled regulars and fine artillery.

The Farmer Boy and How He Became Commander-in-Chief

And thus, my dear children, did this rash and wilful man cast lightly away the golden opportunity, wherein, by a few kind words, or tokens of respect, he could have gained the lasting friendship of this much-despised race, and thereby made them, in all human likelihood, the humble means of saving from early destruction the finest army, which, up to that time, had carried its banners to the Western World.

XV.

ROUGH WORK.

At last, all things were got in readiness; and the gallant little army began its toilsome march through the forest, and over the mountains, and up and down the valleys. Beside the regulars, fourteen hundred strong, it consisted of two companies of hatchet-men, or carpenters, whose business it was to go on before, and open the road; a small company of seamen, who had the care and management of the artillery; six companies of rangers, some of whom were Pennsylvanians; and two companies of light horse, which, being composed of young men taken from the very first families of Virginia, Braddock had chosen to be his body-guard: the whole numbering two thousand, or thereabouts.

Owing to the difficulty of dragging the loaded wagons and heavy guns over the steep and rocky roads, the march was slow and tedious in the extreme; and what made it still more trying to Washington's patience was to see so many wagons and pack-horses loaded down with the private baggage of the English officers,—such as fine clothing, table dainties, and a hundred little troublesome conveniences, which they must needs lug about with them wherever they went. Weeks before they left Fort Cumberland, Washington had pointed out to Braddock the folly of attempting to cross that monstrous mountain barrier with a cumbrous train of wheel-carriages; and expressed the opinion, that, for the present, they had better leave the bulk of their baggage and their heaviest artillery, and, trusting entirely to pack-horses for transporting what should be needed most, make their way at once to Fort Duquesne while the garrison was yet too weak to offer any resistance. This prudent counsel, however, as usual, had failed to produce the least effect on the narrow and stubborn mind of Braddock; but by the time he had dragged his unwieldy length over two or three mountains, and had made but a few miles in many days, it began to dawn on his mind by slow degrees, that a campaign in an American wilderness was a very different thing from what it was in the cultivated regions of Europe, where nearly every meadow, field, or wood, could tell of a Christian and civilized battle there fought, and where the fine roads and bridges made the march of an army a mere holiday jaunt as compared to this rough service. The difficulties that beset him seeming to thicken around him at every step, he was at last so sorely put to it and perplexed as to be obliged to turn to the young provincial colonel for that advice which he, in his blind self-confidence, had but a short while before disdained.

Too well bred to seem surprised at this unbending of the haughty old general, although he really was not a little, Washington readily, yet with all becoming modesty, did as he was desired, in a clear, brief, and soldierly manner. He gave it as his opinion, that their best plan would be to divide the army into two parts,—the smaller division, under command of Col. Dunbar, to form the rear, and bring up the heavy guns and baggage-wagons; the larger division, under the command of Braddock, to form the advance, and taking with it but two pieces of light artillery, and no more baggage than could be conveniently carried on pack-horses, push rapidly on to Fort Duquesne, and surprise the garrison before they could receive timely warning of their danger, or be re-enforced by the troops from Canada, which would have arrived ere then, had not the summer drought prevented. To some extent, this prudent advice was followed; and, to give it the force of example, Washington reduced his baggage to a few little necessaries that he could easily carry in a small portmanteau strapped to his back, and gave his fine charger to be used as a pack-horse. His brother provincial officers, accustomed as they were to dealing with the difficulties and inconveniences of a backwoods life, in a ready, off-hand fashion, followed his example with the greatest willingness and good-humor. Notwithstanding this, however, there were still two hundred pack-horses loaded with the private baggage of the English officers, who were unwilling, even in that hour of pressing need, to make this little sacrifice of their present comfort to the common good. So tender did they seem of their bodily ease, and so given up to the pleasures of appetite, that Washington began to have serious doubts of their fitness to endure the hardships of a rough campaign, and of their courage and firmness to face the dangers of the battle-field.

The Farmer Boy and How He Became Commander-in-Chief

One evening late, about this time, as the army lay encamped at the Little Meadows, there suddenly appeared among them, from the neighboring woods, a large party of hunters, all Pennsylvanians, dressed in the wild garb of Indians, and armed with hatchets, knives, and rifles. Their leader was a certain Capt. Jack, one of the greatest hunters of his day, and nearly as famous in the border tales of Pennsylvania as Daniel Boone in those of green Kentucky. When your Uncle Juvinell was quite a lad, he read the story of this strange man, in an old book, which pleased and interested him so much at the time, that he has never since forgotten it, and will now repeat it to you in the very words of the old chronicler:—

"The 'Black Hunter,' the 'Black Rifle,' the 'Wild Hunter of Juniata,' is a white man. His history is this: He entered the woods with a few enterprising companions, built his cabin, cleared a little land, and amused himself with the pleasure of fishing and hunting. He felt happy; for then he had not a care. But on an evening, when he returned from a day of sport, he found his cabin burnt, his wife and children murdered. From that moment he forsakes civilized man, hunts out caves in which he lives, protects the frontier inhabitants from the Indians, and seizes every opportunity of revenge that offers. He lives the terror of the Indians, and the consolation of the whites. On one occasion, near Juniata, in the middle of a dark night, a family were suddenly awaked from sleep by the report of a gun. They jumped from their huts; and, by the glimmering light from the chimney, saw an Indian fall to rise no more. The open door exposed to view the Wild Hunter. 'I have saved your lives!' he cried; then turned, and was buried in the gloom of night."

Bidding his leather-stockings to wait where they were till he came back, the Black Hunter strode on to the general's tent, and, without more ado than to enter, made known the object of his coming there, in a speech that smacked somewhat of the Indian style of oratory; which I will give you, as nearly as I can, in his own words:—

"Englishmen, the foe is on the watch. He lurks in the strongholds of the mountains. He hides in the shadows of the forest. He hovers over you like a hungry vulture ready to pounce upon its prey. He has made a boast that he will keep his eye upon you, from his look-outs on the hills, day and night, till you have walked into his snare, when he will shoot down your gay red-birds like pigeons. Englishmen, dangers thicken round you at every step; but in the pride of your strength you have blinded your eyes, so that you see them not. I have brought my hunters, who are brave and trusty men, to serve you as scouts and spies. In your front and in your rear, and on either hand, we will scour the woods, and beat the bushes, to stir up the lurking foe, that your gallant men fall not into his murderous ambuscade. To us the secret places of the wilderness are as an open book; in its depths we have made our homes this many a year: there we can find both food and shelter. We ask no pay, and our rifles are all our own."

To this noble and disinterested offer, Braddock returned a cold and haughty answer.

"There is time enough," said he, "for making such arrangements; and I have experienced troops on whom I can rely."

Stung to the quick by this uncivil and ungenerous treatment, the Black Hunter, without another word, turned, and, with a kindling eye and proud step, left the tent. When he told his followers of the scornful manner in which the English general had treated their leader, and rejected their offer of service, they staid not, but, with angry and indignant mien, filed out of the camp, and, plunging once more into the wilderness, left the devoted little army to march on to that destruction to which its ill-starred commander seemed so fatally bent on leading it. The contemptuous indifference which always marked the demeanor of Braddock towards these rude but brave and trusty warriors of the woods was very offensive to Washington; the more, as he knew, that, when it came to be put to the test, these men, unskilled though they were in the modes of civilized warfare, would be found far better fitted to cope with the cunning and stealthy enemy they had then to deal with, than those well-dressed, well-armed, well-drilled, but unwieldy regulars.

After having rested a few days at the Little Meadows, the advanced division of the army once more took up the line of march; but, to Washington's disappointment, made scarcely better speed than before, although lightened of nearly all of the heavy baggage. "I found," wrote he a short time after, "that, instead of pushing on with vigor, we were halting to level every mole-hill, and erect bridges over every brook; by which means we were sometimes four days in getting twelve miles." Slowly the long and straggling lines held on their weary way, now scrambling over some rugged steep, now winding along some narrow defile, till at length the silence of that gloomy vale—the Shades of Death—was again broken by the shouts and uproar of a marching army.

For several days, Washington had been suffering much from fever, attended with a racking headache, which had obliged him to travel in a covered wagon. By the time they reached the great crossings of the Youghiogeny, his illness had so increased, that Dr. Craik, his good friend and physician, declared it would be almost certain death for him to travel further; at the same time advising him to stay where he was until his fever should somewhat abate its violence, when he could come up with Dunbar's rear division. His brother officers also, and even his old general, kindly urged him to give up all thought of going on for the present; while, to render his disappointment more bearable, some of them promised to keep him informed, by writing, of every thing noteworthy which should happen in the course of their march. Seeing then; was no help for it, he suffered himself to be left behind: but it was with a sad and heavy heart that, he saw them pass on without him; and when they had vanished, one by one, in the shadows of the neighboring wilds, and the gleaming of their arms could no longer be seen through the openings of the trees and bushes, he turned with a sigh, and said to the men whom Braddock had left to nurse and guard him, "I would not for five hundred pounds miss being at the taking of Fort Duquesne." Here he lay for ten days; his fever, no doubt, much aggravated by his impatience to rejoin his comrades, and the fear lest he should not be well in time to share with them the dangers and honors of the coming contest.

Meanwhile, Braddock pursued his slow and tedious march, and in a few days had passed the Great Meadows, where young Washington, the year before, as you must well remember, had learned his first lessons in the rude art of war. A few miles beyond this, he came to a deserted Indian camp, on the top of a rocky hill, where, to judge from the number of wigwams, at least one hundred and seventy warriors must have lodged. The fires were still burning; which showed but too plainly that the stealthy foe was on the watch, and not far distant. Some of the trees hard by had been stripped of their bark; and on their white, sappy trunks were to be seen, in the rude picture-writing of the Indians, savage taunts and threats of vengeance meant for the English; while intermixed with these were bullying boasts and blackguard slang, written in the French language, as if to force on the notice of those who were to read them the fact, that there were white as well as red men lurking near.

It had almost slipped my mind to tell you, that Braddock, moved perhaps by the advice of Washington, had, before setting out from Fort Cumberland, employed a small party of Indians, with their sachem Yadi at their head, to serve as guides and spies during the campaign. A few days after passing the deserted camp on the rock, four or five soldiers, straggling too far in the rear, were suddenly waylaid by the prowling foe, and all murdered and scalped on the spot.

To avenge the death of their comrades, a squad of regulars went out in quest of the enemy, and soon came in sight of a small party of Indians, who held up the boughs of trees before them, and stood their rifles on the ground, as a sign that they were friends. Not understanding this, however, and the distance being too great for them to make out who they were, the blundering regulars fired, and one of the party fell dead on the spot,—a youthful warrior, who proved to be the son of the sachem Yadi. When Braddock heard of this melancholy accident, he was deeply grieved. He forthwith sent for the bereaved father, and, to his praise be it ever recorded, endeavored, by kind words and liberal presents, to console him, and make some little amends for his heavy loss; and, as a still further token of his regard, he ordered the hapless youth to be buried with all the honors of war. The body, borne on a bier, was followed by the officers, two and two; while the soldiers, drawn up in two lines, with the grave between them, stood facing each other, with the points of their muskets turned downward, and their chins resting in the hollow of the breeches. When the body was lowered, they fired three volleys over the grave, and left the young warrior to his long sleep on the hillside, with his bright hatchet and trusty rifle beside him. All this was very soothing to the sorrow and gratifying to the fatherly pride of the old sachem, and made him ever after a loving friend and faithful ally of the English. I have told you this little story to show you, that this testy and obstinate old general, with all his faults, was far from being the hard, unfeeling man that he sometimes seemed; and also as a tribute that every historian should pay to the memory of one whose misfortune it has been to be blamed so much, and pitied so little.

By this time, Washington had so far regained his strength as to admit of his being borne along in a covered wagon; and, setting out accordingly, in five days came up with the advance division, where it lay encamped in a beautiful spot about two miles from the Monongahela, and fifteen miles from Fort Duquesne. Here he was joyfully welcomed by both officers and men, with whom his generosity, and frank, manly bearing, had made him a great favorite. Shortly after his arrival, Mr. Gist and two Indian scouts, who had been sent out to reconnoitre or spy out the enemy, came back with the cheering tidings, that the re-enforcements had not yet come down from Canada, and that the garrison in the fort was at present too weak to stand a single hour's siege. But what gave him a little uneasiness was a lofty column of smoke, rising from a deep and densely wooded hollow, where they were quite sure the watchful enemy was lurking, and hatching some mischief for the English.

Now, the fort and the camp lay on the same side of the river; and the most direct route between them was by a narrow mountain pass, rising abruptly from the water's edge on the left, and, on the right, shut in by a steep and lofty hill, whose stony sides were overgrown with laurel and stunted cedars and pines. As it was altogether out of the question to drag their wagons and artillery along this pass, it was resolved to cross the river, first at a point just over against the camp, and then, moving down along the opposite bank, recross it at another point five miles below; at both of which places the fords were shallow, and the banks not high.

At last, the 9th of July, 1755,—a day ever to be remembered in American annals,—began to dawn. Long before its first red light had streaked the east, a hum in the camp told that the little army was, even at that hour, all astir, and big with the bustle of preparation. Officers and men were in the highest hopes, and looked forward with confidence to the coming evening, when they were to plant their victorious banners on the ramparts of Fort Duquesne. Although they had marched thus far without serious molestation, yet Col. Washington's fears of an ambuscade were not a whit diminished; for he felt quite certain that they should never reach the French fort without an attempt being made to surprise, or drive them back. Full of these apprehensions, he went to Gen. Braddock, and, pointing out to him the danger hanging over them, urged him by all means to send out the Virginia rangers to scour the woods and thickets, front and flank, and beat up the enemy, should any chance to be lurking near with the design of drawing them into an ambuscade. No advice, as it afterwards turned out, could have been more timely: but, coming from a raw provincial colonel, Braddock cast it aside with angry impatience; and when the line of march was formed, as if to show in what light esteem he held it, he ordered the rangers to the rear, to guard the baggage. Before daybreak, a large party of pioneers, or road-cutters, with a small guard of regulars, numbering in all about three hundred, had gone on before to open a passage for the army through the woods, and make the fords more passable by levelling the banks.

The midsummer sun was shooting its first beams, level and red, among the Alleghany hills, when the little army, having crossed the Monongahela at the upper ford, stood on its southern bank, forming in line of march. By order of their general, officers and men had scoured and polished their arms and accoutrements the night before; and now appeared in full uniform, as if some grand military parade were to be the programme of the day. The whole line was soon moving slowly forward, with fifes playing, drums beating, and colors flying; the regulars keeping step the while to the "Grenadier's March." In the clear and tranquil depths of the river, as they moved along its shady banks, could be seen, as in a mirror, the long array of leather-shirted rangers and red-coated regulars, with their sun-lit arms and prancing steeds, and bright banners that floated in the morning breeze. This brilliant spectacle, so well set off by the smiling river in front and the frowning woods beyond, formed a picture that ever lived in the memory of Washington; and in after-years he used

The Farmer Boy and How He Became Commander-in-Chief

often to say, that, as it then appeared to him, he thought he had never seen any thing so beautiful. In the enthusiasm of the moment, he forgot his late illness, the still enfeebled condition of his body, — all, save the glory of serving his country; and, mounting his horse, he joined his brother-aides in their attendance on their general, else far more fatal must have been the end of that bloody day.

XVI.

BRADDOCK'S DEFEAT.

In my account of this battle, as well as all the others that will come thundering in upon us from time to time in the course of our story, I have thought it would suit our purpose best to touch upon those facts only that are likeliest to leave the most lasting pictures of such events on your minds; using the while no more words than may actually be needed to give clearness and completeness to the same. And now, Daniel, my young Herodotus, and Ned, my young Hannibal, bring in another Christmas log, that we may have a more cheerful blaze; for our story will be doleful enough for the next half-hour, without these goblin shadows dodging and flitting about the room to make it more so.

At mid-day, Braddock's army came to the lower ford, where a halt was called to allow of a few minutes' rest. Far in front, across the river, the ringing of a hundred axes, followed at short intervals by the crash of falling trees, could be distinctly heard; telling that the pioneers were there, working might and main to clear a passage for those behind. The road just opened, after leaving the ford, ran across a heavily wooded bottom that skirted the river; and thence, for a few hundred yards, up a rocky slope to the foot of a high range of hills, about a mile distant, where it entered a narrow, bushy defile, and went no further. The country, for miles and miles around, as far as the eye could reach, was thickly wooded, save the rocky slope just mentioned, and the neighboring ravines, which were overgrown with long, coarse grass and whortleberry-bushes, so high as to sweep the horses' bellies; with here and there a few scattering trees of some size. It was the very place, of all others, that the wily Indian would be most likely to choose for his ambuscade.

By two o'clock, the whole army had regained the northern bank of the river. They were now within ten miles of Fort Duquesne, and a lucky end to their present campaign seemed near at hand. In a few minutes, artillery and baggage, foot and horse, regulars and rangers, formed into separate and distinct columns, stood ready to move as soon as the word should be given. Just at the moment, however, when they were listening to hear the order, "Forward, march!" drop from their general's lips, they were startled by a sudden and heavy firing among the hills, which put a sudden stop to the hundred axes, and told but too plainly that the road-cutters and their guard of regulars had been drawn into an ambuscade. Washington knew at once, and too well, that the evil he dreaded from the beginning, had, on the very eve of success, come upon them; and with it also came the painful reflection, that it would never have so befallen them, had the rangers been suffered to scour the woods, and beat up the enemy, as had been recommended by him but a few hours before. Braddock forthwith ordered two companies to hurry on to the relief of the pioneers; and, at his bidding, one of his aides spurred forward to learn further of the matter, and bring him word. The firing grew heavier and heavier, and seemed to be coming nearer and nearer. The lonely hills and woods around rang with the whoops and yells of the unseen savages. Not able to restrain his impatience till his aide came back, Braddock ordered his main division to come up at double-quick; and, taking with him his two remaining aides and a small guard of light-horse, galloped up to the scene of action. Here what was his rage and mortification to find his doughty regulars, of whom he had boasted so much, changed, as it were in the whistling of a bullet, into a mere disorderly rabble of red-coats,—confused, bewildered, to a degree that he could never have dreamed possible! Crowded and huddled together in the narrow road, he saw them dropping down under the Indian bullets, helpless as a herd of frightened deer beset by a band of unseen hunters.

By this time, the Indians, still hid from view by the grass and bushes, had stretched their lines along either side of the road, from the hollows among the hills to some distance down the rocky slope, and were pouring in a murderous fire upon the affrighted English; yelling and whooping the while like a legion of devils at some infernal frolic. Two bayonet charges had been made to drive them from their hiding-places, but in vain. The regulars, notwithstanding their officers' orders to the contrary, kept up a hurried but random firing, which had little or no effect upon the enemy, as nothing could be seen of him but the puffs of rifle-smoke that rose and hovered in little blue clouds over his place of ambush. The English, it is said, were less appalled by the whistling bullet; of the unseen savages than by their unearthly yells,—a sound that none of them had ever heard before, and many a poor fellow of them never heard again. The Indian war-whoop has been described as a sound so wild and terrible, that, when once heard in battle, it rings in the listener's ears for weeks thereafter, and is never forgotten even to his dying day.

But the English officers, on the contrary, behaved themselves with a gallantry that filled Washington with astonishment and admiration. Heretofore he had seen them only in camp or on the line of march, where their habits of ease and self-indulgence had led him to doubt their having the courage and firmness to face, without shrinking, danger in such appalling forms. Unmindful of the bullets that whistled continually about their heads, they galloped up and down the broken and bleeding lines, in the vain endeavor to rally their men, and bring them again to something like order. Mounted on fine horses, and dressed in rich uniforms, they offered a tempting mark to the unseen rifles that were levelled at them from behind every tree and bush, and tuft of grass; and, ere the work of death was finished, many a gallant steed, with dangling reins and bloody saddle, dashed riderless about the field. And, as if this were not enough, many of them must needs fall victims to the unsoldierly conduct of their own men, who, forgetful of all discipline, and quite beside themselves with terror and bewilderment, loaded their pieces hurriedly, and fired them off at random, killing friends as well as foes. Nor did this most shameful part of the bloody scene end here: many of the Virginia rangers, who had already taken to the trees and bushes, and were doing good service by fighting the Indians in their own fashion, were shot down by the blundering regulars, who fired into the woods wherever they saw a puff of smoke, unable to distinguish whether it rose from a red or a white man's rifle. Upon these brave rangers the brunt of the battle fell; and indeed, had it not been for their firmness and presence of mind, their skill and address in the arts and stratagems of Indian warfare, which enabled them for a time to hold the enemy in check, hardly a remnant of Braddock's fine army would have survived to behold the going-down of that summer's sun.

The Farmer Boy and How He Became Commander-in-Chief

At the very commencement of the battle, a small party of warriors, cheered on by a French officer in a fancifully trimmed hunting-shirt, had leaped out from their covert into the road, with the view, it seemed, of cutting off those in front from the assistance of their comrades in the rear; but the regulars, who guarded the road-cutters, having discharged a well-aimed volley of musketry into their very faces, they had turned, and fled with even more haste than they had come, leaving behind them several of their number dead on the spot, and among these their dashing French leader. After that, they had taken care to keep close under cover of the grass and bushes. Now and then, however, a tall brave, grim and hideous with war-paint, with a yell of defiance would leap from his ambush, and, darting into the road, tomahawk and scalp a wounded officer just fallen; then vanish again as suddenly as if the earth had opened to swallow him up.

All this while, Col. Washington had borne himself with a firmness, courage, and presence of mind, that would have done honor to a forty-years' veteran. His two brother aides-de-camp having been wounded early in the engagement, the whole duty of carrying the general's orders had fallen on him; and nobly did he that day discharge it. Although brave men were falling thick and fast on every side, yet he shrank from no exposure, however perilous, did his duty but lead him there. Mounted on horseback, his tall and stately form was to be seen in every part of the field, the mark of a hundred rifles, whose deadly muzzles were pointed at him whithersoever he went. Two horses were shot dead under him, and his coat was pierced with bullets; but he seemed to bear about him a charmed life, and went unharmed. His danger was so great, that his friend Dr. Craik, who watched his movements with anxious interest, looked every moment to see him fall headlong to the ground; and that he came off alive seemed to him a miracle. Washington himself, with that piety which ever marked his character, laid his deliverance from the perils of that fatal day to the overruling care of a kind and watchful Providence.

Although brought thus suddenly face to face with new and untried dangers, Braddock bore himself throughout the day like the valiant man that he really was. The bullets and yells of the invisible foe he scarcely noticed, as he galloped hither and thither about the field, giving his orders through a speaking-trumpet, whose brazen voice rose loud and hoarse above the din of battle. Under the mistaken notion that a savage enemy, hid in a thicket, was to be dealt with as a civilized one in an open plain, he sought to recover his lost ground by forming his men into companies and battalions; which, however, he had no sooner done, than they were mowed down by the murderous fire from the ambush, that had never ceased. "My soldiers," said he, "would fight, could they but see their enemy; but it is vain to shoot at trees and bushes." Whereupon Washington urgently besought him to let his regulars fight the Indians in their own fashion, which would the better enable them to pick off the lurking foe with less danger to their own safety. But Braddock's only answer to this was a sneer; and some of his regulars, who were already acting upon the suggestion, he angrily ordered back into the ranks, calling them cowards, and even striking them with the flat of his sword. He then caused the colors of the two regiments to be advanced in different parts of the field, that the soldiers might rally around their separate standards. It was all in vain. In his excitement, he cheered, he entreated, he swore, he stormed: it was only a waste of breath; for the poor fellows were too disheartened and broken, too overcome by mortal fear, to rally again.

Col. Washington, seeing that the day was on the point of being lost, galloped down to the rear to see if nothing could be done with the artillery; but he found the gunners in a most disorderly plight, benumbed with terror, and utterly unable to manage their guns. What Washington did on this occasion, I had better tell you in the words of an old Pennsylvania soldier, who was there at the time, and survived the battle for half a hundred years or more; and used often, for the entertainment of your Uncle Juvinell and other little boys, to fight his battles over again as he sat smoking in his chimney corner.

"I saw Col. Washington," he would say, "spring from his panting horse, and seize a brass field-piece as if it had been a stick. His look was terrible. He put his right hand on the muzzle, his left hand on the breech; he pulled with this, he pushed with that, and wheeled it round, as if it had been a plaything: it furrowed the ground like a ploughshare. He tore the sheet-lead from the touch-hole; then the powder-monkey rushed up with the fire, when the cannon went off, making the bark fly from the trees, and many an Indian send up his last yell and bite the dust."

This, however, gave the savages but a momentary check, as he could not follow it up; there being no one by ready and willing to lend him a helping hand. The Virginia rangers and other provincial troops, who had done the only good fighting of the day, were thinned out to one-fourth their number; and the few that remained were too weary and faint to hold out longer against such fearful odds. Between the well-aimed firing of the enemy and the random shooting of the regulars, the slaughter of the English officers had been frightful: out of the eighty-six who went into the battle, only twenty-four came off unhurt. Gen. Braddock had five horses killed under him. By this time, he had given up all hope of regaining the day; and, galling as it must have been to his proud spirit, was at last forced to think of retreating as their only chance of safety. Just as he was on the point, however, of giving orders to this effect, a bullet—said by some to have been a random shot from one of his own soldiers—passed through his arm, and, lodging itself in his lungs, brought him to the ground, mortally wounded. His officers placed him in a tumbrel, or pioneer's cart, and bore him from the field, where, in his despair, he prayed them to leave him to die.

Seeing their leader fall, a fresh panic seized the army. And now followed a wild and disorderly rout, the like of which was never known before, and has never since been known, in our border-wars. The soldiers in front fell back on those in the centre; those in the centre fell back on those in the rear: till foot and horse, artillery and baggage, were jammed and jumbled together, making a scene of dismay and confusion it would be vain for me to attempt to describe. To add wings to their speed, the Indians, with a long, loud yell of fiendish triumph, now rushed from their ambush, and, brandishing aloft their murderous tomahawks, began to press hard on the heels of the terrified fugitives. The better to elude their savage pursuers, the regulars threw away their arms, the gunners abandoned their guns, and the teamsters cut their horses from the traces, and, mounting them, fled, never halting until they reached Col. Dunbar's camp,—a gallop of forty miles. A few fell under the tomahawk before the farther bank of the river could be gained. Here, luckily for the survivors, the Indians gave over the pursuit, in their eagerness to plunder the slain, and gather what else of booty might be found on the field.

Thus ended this bloody battle, or rather slaughter; for in truth it could be called nothing else. Of the sixteen hundred valiant men who had that morning, in all the bright array of gleaming arms and waving banners, marched along the banks of that beautiful river, nearly one-half, ere the sun went down, had fallen on Braddock's Hill. What made this disaster more shameful still was the weakness of the enemy's force, which did not exceed eight hundred, of whom only a fourth were French; and, of all this number, scarcely forty fell in the fight.

Col. Washington was now ordered to ride back with all speed to Dunbar's camp, to fetch horses, wagons, and hospital-stores for the relief of the wounded. Although still quite weak from his ten days' fever, which indeed had left him with no more strength than should have sufficed for the fatigues of that trying day, yet he set out on the instant, and, taking with him a guard of grenadiers, travelled the livelong night. What with those terrible sights and sounds still ringing in his ears, and flashing before his eyes; what with the thought of the many dead and dying that lay on the lonely hillside far behind, with their ghastly upturned faces, more ghastly still in the light of the moon; and what with the bitter, bitter reflection, that all this would never have been but for the pride and folly of a single man,—that ride through the dark and silent woods must have been a melancholy one indeed. He pushed on, without leaving the saddle, till late in the afternoon of the following day, when he reached Dunbar's camp; and gathering together, without loss of time, the necessaries for which he had been sent, started on his return that same night, scarcely allowing himself and men an hour for food and rest. Early next morning, he met the main division at Mr. Gist's plantation, whither they had dragged their shattered lines the evening before. From thence they all went on together to the Great Meadows, where they arrived that same day, and halted.

The Farmer Boy and How He Became Commander-in-Chief

For the four and twenty hours following the battle, Braddock had remained sad and silent; never speaking except to say, "Who would have thought it?" The second day, he seemed more cheerful; for he said, "We shall better know how to deal with them another time." He spoke in high praise of the skill and courage shown by the Virginia rangers and other provincial troops during the whole engagement. He now saw, but too late, and to his deep regret, that he had not given these rough and hardy men half the credit due them as good soldiers; and also that he had made a fatal mistake in underrating the strength, skill, and address of the enemy he had been sent there to subdue. To Washington he made a frank and manly apology for the contempt and impatience with which he had so often treated his prudent and well-timed counsel. As if wishing to make still further amends for this, he bequeathed to him his faithful negro servant, Bishop, and his fine white charger, both of whom had helped to carry their wounded master from the field. On the fourth day after the battle, he died; having been kindly and tenderly cared for by Washington and his other surviving officers.

They dug him a grave by the roadside, not a stone's-throw from Fort Necessity, in the depths of that lonely wilderness; and there, before the summer morn had dawned, they buried him. In the absence of the chaplain, the funeral service was read by Washington, in a low and solemn voice, by the dim and flickering light of a torch. Fearing lest the enemy might be lurking near, and, spying out the spot, commit some outrage on his remains, they fired not a farewell shot over the grave of their unfortunate general,—that last tribute of respect to a departed soldier, and one he had himself paid, but a short time before, to a nameless Indian warrior. So there they laid him; and, to this day, the great highway leading from Cumberland to Pittsburg goes by the name of Braddock's Road.

I would, my dear children, have you dwell on these glimpses of a more manly and generous nature that brightened the closing hours of Braddock's life; because it is but Christian and just that we should be willing to honor virtue in whomsoever it may be found. With all his self-conceit and obstinacy, he had a kindly heart, and was a brave man; and had it been his lot to deal with a civilized enemy, instead of a savage one, he would, no doubt, have proved himself a skilful general. And we should not deal too harshly with the memory of a man, whose faults, however great they may have been, were more than atoned for by the inglorious death he died, and by "a name ever coupled with defeat."

XVII.

EXPLANATIONS.

Here, again, Uncle Juvinell paused in his story, and looked beamingly around on his little auditors. They were all sitting with their eyes bent earnestly on the burning logs, thinking deeply, no doubt, and looking as sober as tombstones in the light of a spring morning.

All on a sudden, Willie leaped from his chair, and gave a shrill Indian war-whoop, that threw the whole bevy into a terrible panic; making some of the smaller fry scream outright, and even Uncle Juvinell to blink a little. "There," said the youngster, "is something to ring in your ears for weeks hereafter, and never to be forgotten even to your dying day. I heard it the other night at the Indian circus, and have been practising it myself ever since. I fancy it must be a pretty fair sample of the genuine thing, or it wouldn't have scared you all up as it did." Whereupon Uncle Juvinell, frowning over his spectacles with his brows, and laughing behind them with his eyes, bade the young blood to pack himself into his chair again, and be civil; at the same time threatening to put him on a water-gruel diet, to bring his surplus spirits within reasonable bounds. Then all the little folks laughed, not so much at what their uncle had said, as to make believe they had not been frightened in the least; in which Willie, the cunning rogue, joined, that, under cover of the general merriment, he might snicker a little to himself at his own smartness.

"And now, my dear children," continued the good man, "hand me the notes you have written down, that I may see what it is you would have me explain."

"In five minutes' time after you began," said rattle-brained Willie, "I became so much interested in the story, that I quite forgot all about the notes, till it was too late to begin; but I was thinking all along, that I should like to understand more clearly the difference between a province and a colony, and" —

"Indeed, uncle," broke in Dannie, "you made every thing so clear and plain as you went along, that I, for one, didn't feel the need of writing down a single note."

"Then, Dannie," said his uncle, "that being the case, you can perhaps enlighten your cousin Willie as to the difference between a colony and a province."

Had his uncle called upon him to give the difference between Gog and Magog, Daniel would have made the venture. So he promptly answered,—

"A province is a country, and a colony is the people of it."

Uncle Juvinell would have laughed outright at this answer; but he knew it would mortify the young historian: so he only smiled, and said,—

"That will do pretty well, Dannie, as far as it goes; but it does not cover more than an acre of the ground. Now, a colony, you must know, Willie, is a settlement made by a country—called, in such cases, the mother-country—in some foreign region at a distance from it, but belonging to it; as, for example, the English colonies in America, which are separated from the mother-country, England, by the great Atlantic Ocean. A province, on the other hand, is a similar extent of foreign territory, belonging to a nation or a kingdom, either by conquest or purchase or settlement; and it may also be a division or district of the kingdom or nation itself. Thus, you see, a foreign region, settled and owned by the mother-country, may, with nearly equal propriety, be called either a colony or a province; while one that belongs to a nation or a kingdom by conquest or purchase is a province, and nothing else. Thus, for example, Canada is a province of Great Britain, won from the French by conquest, as you will learn to-morrow evening. From this you may see, that although a province may, yet a colony can no more exist within the boundaries of a mother-country, than can a man live at home and abroad at one and the same time."

The other children were then called on to produce their notes. Laura said, that, after she had written two or three, she found she was losing more than she was gaining; for, when she stopped to take down any item she wished to remember, she did not hear what came right after. Ellen chimed in with the same; and Ned said he was not yet out of his pot-hooks, and couldn't write; but that he was thinking all the time of getting Willie or Dannie to tell him all about it after they went to bed. So, what with this excuse, and that, and the other, not a single note was forthcoming, except a few that Master Charlie, the knowing young gentleman, had written on a very large slate, in letters quite of his own inventing, which he now laid before his uncle. To set off his penmanship to the best advantage, and couple the ornamental with the useful, he had drawn just above it a picture of Gen. Braddock, mounted on his dashing white charger, and waving aloft a sword of monstrous length. One unacquainted with the subject, however, would sooner have taken it for a big baboon, geared up in a cocked hat and high military boots, with a mowing-scythe in his hand, and astraddle of a rearing donkey heavily coated with feathers instead of hair. The old gentleman's spectacles seemed to twinkle as he ran his eye over the slate; and after making out two or three rather savage-looking *s*'s, as many long-legged *p*'s, a squat *h* or two, a big bottle-bellied *b*, three or four gigantic *l*'s, a broken-backed *k* or two, a high-shouldered *w*, a heavy-bottomed *d*, and a long slim-tailed *y*, it struck him, at length, that speech-belt, Long Knife, knapsack, Silver Heels, wigwam, and powder-monkey, were the items concerning which Master Charlie desired further enlightenment.

"For information touching these matters, my dear Charles," then said Uncle Juvinell, "I will pass you over to Willie and Dannie, who, I dare say, are quite as well posted up in matters of this kind, as your old uncle; for, if I mistake not, they have just been reading Catlin's book on the Indians, and Gulliver's Travels in Brobdignag."

"How is it," inquired Ellen, "that Washington, being the good man that he was, could have taken part in that wicked war between the French and English about a country that didn't belong to either of them, but to the poor Indians?"

Now, although Uncle Juvinell was satisfied in his own mind that Washington's conduct in this matter was just what it should have been, yet, for all that, he was a little puzzled how to answer this question in a way that the little folks would rightly understand.

"This very thing, my dear niece," replied he after a moment's pause, "grieved and troubled his mind a great deal, as you may well believe: but he knew, that, if the English did not get possession of this land, the French would; and this, by increasing the strength of the enemy, would by and by endanger the safety of his own native land, and even the lives and liberties of his countrymen. And he also knew that it would be far better for the spread of useful knowledge and the true religion, that all this rich country should be in the hands of some Christian people, who would make it a place fit to live in, and to be peaceful and prosperous and happy in, than that it should be left entirely to those barbarous savages, who only made of it a place to hunt and to fish in, to fight and scalp, and to burn and torture each other like devils in. Besides this, it is the duty of every true patriot (and no one knew this better than he) to serve and defend the country, under the protection of whose laws he has lived in peace and plenty, against all her enemies, whether at home or abroad, even should she now and then be a little in the wrong; for, by so doing, he defends his own home and family, rights and liberty,—objects that should be as dear to him as life itself."

"O uncle!" exclaimed Ned with a start, as if he had just caught a passing recollection by the tail as it was about skedaddling round the corner, "tell me, will you? what kind of a life a charmed life is."

"Really Ned," cried Uncle Juvinell, "I am very glad that you mentioned it; for it puts me in mind of something I should have told you before, and which I might else have forgotten. This, however, is as good a time as any; and, when you hear what I am now going to tell you, you will readily understand, without further explanation, what is meant when it is said of a man that he bears a charmed life about him. To do this, I must anticipate a little, or, to speak more clearly, take time by the forelock, and, going forward a little in our story, tell you of a circumstance which your Uncle Juvinell, when a boy, often heard related by Dr. Craik, who was then an aged and venerable man.

"Fifteen years after poor Braddock had been laid in his unhonored grave, Col. Washington, taking with him his friend Dr. Craik, went on an exploring expedition to the Ohio, in behalf of the brave soldiers who had served under him at the Great Meadows, and to whom, it must be remembered, Gov. Dinwiddie had promised two hundred thousand acres of the best land to be found on this great river or its branches. There was peace then along the border, and little or no danger was to be apprehended from the Indians. They travelled in a large canoe, rowed by two or three hunters; and what with fishing in the streams (for they took with them their fishing tackle), what with hunting in the woods (for they took with them their hunting rifles), what with camping on the green shore at night (for they took with them their camp utensils), and what with the comfortable thought that there was not an Indian warrior within a hundred miles whose fingers were itching for their scalps (for they took with them this and many other pleasant thoughts besides), they had, you may depend upon it, a glorious time.

"One day, there came to their camp, at the mouth of the Great Kanawha, a party of Indians, headed by an old chief of grave and venerable aspect, who approached Washington with deep reverence, as if entering the presence of some superior being. After several pipes of tobacco had been smoked, and several haunches of venison had been eaten,—the first to show that they had come friendly, the last to show that they came hungry,—the old chief addressed Washington in a speech, which your Uncle Juvinell cannot repeat to you word for word as he heard it from the lips of the worthy old doctor; but he well remembers the substance thereof, and will give it you as nearly as he can in the Indian style of oratory.

"'They came and told me,' began the old chief, 'that the great Long Knife was in our country; and I was very glad. I said to them, though I be old and feeble, though the way be long, and the hills many and high, and the rivers many and wide, yet must I go and see him once more before I die; for it is the young warrior, whom, years ago, I saw shielded from our bullets by the hand of the Great Spirit. Let the pale-faces hear my words. Fifteen summers ago, when the woods and thickets were dense and green, the French and Indians went out to lay in ambuscade for the big English general, among the

The Farmer Boy and How He Became Commander-in-Chief

Monongahela hills. I took my warriors, and went along, and we lay in wait together. The English were many and strong; we were few and weak: thus we had no thought of victory in our minds, but only to give our enemies a little trouble, and keep them back a while till the big French army came down from the Great Lakes. We saw the English army cross the river and come up the hill; yet they suspected not. We saw them walk into our snare, up to the very muzzles of our guns; nor did they dream of danger, till our war-whoop went up, and our bullets began to fly as fast as winter hail. I saw the red-coats fall, and strew the ground like the red leaves of the woods nipped by an untimely frost, and smitten by the unseen hands of a mighty wind. The snows of eighty winters have fallen upon my head. I have been in many a bloody battle; yet never saw I the red life-stream run as it that day ran down Braddock's Hill from English hearts. Listen! I saw that day, among the English, a young warrior who was not an Englishman. I singled him out as a mark for my rifle; for he was tall and strong, and rode grandly, and his presence there was a danger to us. Seventeen times did I take slow and steady aim, and fire; but my bullets went astray, and found him not. Then I pointed him out to my young men, whose eyes were sharper and whose hands were steadier than mine, and bade them bring him down. It was all in vain: their bullets glanced from him as if he had been a rock. I saw two horses fall under him, shot dead; yet he rose unhurt. Then did I lay my hand on my mouth in wonder, and bade my young men turn their rifles another way; for the Great Spirit, I knew, held that young warrior in his keeping, and that his anger would be kindled against us if we desisted not. That young warrior, the favorite of Heaven, the man who is destined never to fall in battle, now stands before me. Once more mine eyes have seen him, and I shall now go away content.'

"And now, Ned, my boy," said Uncle Juvinell, after he had ended this oration, "can you tell me what a charmed life is?"

"One that is bullet-proof, I suppose," replied Ned.

"You don't mean to say that Washington was bullet-proof, do you, Uncle Juve?" put in doubting Charlie.

"No, not exactly that, my little nephew," replied his Uncle Juvinell; "and yet a great deal more: for, beyond all doubt, an all-wise Providence raised up George Washington to do the good and great work that he did, and to this end shielded him when encompassed by the perils of battle, strengthened him when beset by the wiles of temptation, and cheered him when visited by the trials of adversity. Dr. Davis, a famous preacher of that day, seemed to have looked upon him, as did the old Indian, as one favored of Heaven; for, in a sermon preached by him a few weeks after Braddock's defeat, he spoke of Col. Washington as 'that heroic youth, whom, he could not but hope, Providence had preserved in so signal a manner for some important service to his country.' And now, my little folks, the clock strikes nine, and our Christmas logs burn low: so join your old uncle in an evening hymn; then haste you to your happy beds to sleep and dream the peaceful night away."

XVIII.

WORK IN EARNEST.

Hardly had the last clod been thrown on poor Braddock's grave, when his army was seized with a second and most unaccountable panic; for no one could tell from whence or how it came. With those horrid yells still sounding in their ears, and those ghastly sights of blood and carnage still fresh in their memories, they fancied they heard, in every passing gust that stirred the dead leaves, warning whispers of the stealthy approach of the dreaded enemy, and that in every waving thicket he might be lurking for them in ambush.

Col. Dunbar, as next in rank, had, for the time being, taken command of the troops; but, cowardly as the old general was rash, he shared in the general panic, and could do nothing to re-assure his men or give them a little confidence. So, without waiting to know by whose orders, or if by any at all, they fell to, and destroyed all the heavy baggage, baggage-wagons, and artillery; every thing, in fact, that could hinder them in their retreat. Thus disencumbered, they set out in hot haste; and after a hurried and disorderly march, or rather flight, they reached Fort Cumberland.

Here Col. Washington, who had taken no part whatever in the unsoldierly proceedings just mentioned, stopped a few days to recruit a little after the severe fatigues he had, for a week past, been called upon to undergo, while still too much enfeebled from his ten-days' fever. The first use he made of this breathing spell was to write an affectionate letter to his much-honored mother to ease her mind of the anxiety he knew she would be feeling on his account, when rumors of the late disaster should reach her ears. He told her of his almost miraculous deliverance from a cruel and bloody death, in language full of gratitude to the God of battles, who had shielded him in so signal a manner, when his brave comrades were falling by hundreds around him. Writing to his brother Augustine at the same time, he wittily says, "Since my arrival at this place, I have heard a circumstantial account of my death and dying speech; and I take this early opportunity of contradicting the former, and assuring you that I have not yet composed the latter."

When he had so far regained his strength as to enable him to travel, he betook himself once more to the peaceful shades of Mount Vernon. He re-entered at once upon his duties as Adjutant-General of the Northern District,—a post he still continued to hold, although his connection with the regular army had ceased with the death of Braddock.

But we must return for a few moments to Fort Cumberland, where we left the valorous Col. Dunbar quite out of breath from the uncommonly brisk speed, which seems to have been his habit now and then, of getting over very rough and hilly roads. Any soldier, with a spark of manly spirit under his sword-belt, would have made a resolute stand at a place of so much importance, and held it to the death, rather than left the defenceless inhabitants exposed to the horrors of a border war. Col. Dunbar was not, by any means, the true soldier just hinted at; and consequently did no such thing. Seeing that the sick and wounded were but so many clogs to rapid and easy motion, he resolved to leave them behind under the care of the slender garrison he had placed in the fort, who were expected to defend it against an enemy that he, with a force of fifteen hundred strong, had not the courage to face. Thus rid of his hinderances to the last degree of lightsomeness, he pushed on by forced marches, as if a legion of painted savages were yelling at his heels; and never slackened speed until he found himself safe within the friendly walls of Philadelphia, where he went into comfortable winter-quarters while yet the dog-days were at their hottest.

Thus basely deserted by these doughty regulars, who had been sent over so many thousand miles of salt water for their protection, the colonists saw with dismay the whole line of their vast frontier, from Lake Ontario to the Carolinas, open to the inroads of the French and their Indian allies. In the long-run, however (as you shall see hereafter), two luckier mishaps than Braddock's defeat and Dunbar's retreat, that seemed at the time so fraught with evil, could not have befallen them. They were thereby taught two wholesome lessons, which they might otherwise have been a long time in learning, and without which they never could have gained their independence and made themselves a nation. The first, by proving that British regulars were not, by any means, the never-to-be-beaten, and the never-to-be-made-to-skedaddle warriors that they boasted themselves to be, and that one-half of the Americans were foolish enough to believe them to be. Thus, when the War of Independence broke out, our Revolutionary fathers remembered this, and were not afraid to meet the English even on such unequal terms. The second, by opening their eyes to the fact, that, as they (the colonists) could no longer look to the mother-country for protection, they must henceforward rely upon their own strength and resources for their defence and safety.

The people of Virginia, seeing the forlorn condition of things, were at last awakened to a full sense of the danger that threatened, not only their back settlements, but even the heart of the Old Dominion itself. They therefore began to bestir themselves in right good earnest to put the province in a better posture of defence; and, to this end, resolved to send more troops into the field, raise more money, procure new arms and fresh supplies of military stores, and erect a chain of twenty block-houses, or small forts, stretching along the whole line of their frontier, from Pennsylvania to North Carolina,—a distance of three hundred and sixty miles. Washington's career as a soldier had not, up to this time, been marked by any of those daring and brilliant exploits that charm and dazzle vulgar minds; but had, on the contrary, been one unbroken train of misfortunes and disasters. Notwithstanding this, however, the confidence his countrymen had placed in his prudence, courage, ability, and patriotism, so far from having been diminished thereby, had gone on steadily gaining strength from the very beginning. They well knew, that, had the headstrong and unlucky Braddock given heed to his prudent and timely counsel, the late campaign could never have ended in the disgraceful and disastrous manner that it had. As the most flattering proof of their esteem and confidence, they now turned to him in their hour of peril, and, although he was not yet twenty-four years of age, called upon him, as with one voice, to take the chief command of all the forces of the province. After some deliberation, being persuaded that it was really their earnest desire, he modestly accepted the appointment, on condition that certain changes should be made in the military, and that he should be allowed to choose his field-officers. This was readily agreed to by the Virginia House of Burgesses; who, in addition, voted him fifteen hundred dollars by way of compensating him for the many losses he had suffered, in horses, baggage, and money since the beginning of the war.

Accordingly, early in the autumn, he took up his headquarters at the frontier town of Winchester, beyond the Blue Ridge, in the beautiful Valley of the Shenandoah. As four great highways met here from as many different quarters of the country, it was a post of much importance; and he resolved, by strongly fortifying it, to make it the rallying-point of all the border. His men were all raw recruits, just taken from the plough or forge or carpenter's bench, as the case might be; and, to render them fit for the peculiar service in which they were to be employed, it became his duty, besides training them in the regular military exercises, to instruct them in the arts and stratagems of Indian warfare, or bush-fighting, as it is more aptly called. Long, however, before he was ready to take the field, the French and Indians, made daring and audacious by their great victory on the Monongahela, had crossed the mountains at several different points in great numbers, and had already begun their bloody work. The terrified and defenceless inhabitants dwelling in the distant parts of the wilderness now came flocking to the Shenandoah Valley for protection from the merciless enemy, some of them never stopping till they had passed on over to the eastern slopes of the Blue Ridge.

One morning, a rumor found its way to Winchester, that a large party of Indians were within twelve miles of that place, pillaging, burning, and murdering at a frightful rate. Straightway a great fear fell upon the inhabitants. Little children ran, and hid their faces in their mothers' aprons, crying piteously; women ran hither and thither, screaming, and wringing their hands; and broad-shouldered, double-fisted men stood stock-still, and shook in their moccasins. Washington tried to prevail upon some of his soldiers to sally out with him, and drive the enemy back from the valley; but, being strangers to military obedience, not a leather-shirt of all the rabble could he get to venture beyond the ditches. When he put them in mind of what was expected of them as men and soldiers, they only answered, that, if they must die, they would rather stay there, and die with their wives and families. Having a lurking suspicion, that, after all, there might be more smoke than fire in these flying rumors, he sent out a scout to bring him some more certain tidings of the matter. In a wonderfully short time, the scout came back, pale and affrighted, with the dismal intelligence that he had, with his own ears, heard the guns and yells of the Indians not four miles distant, and that Winchester would be beset by the savages in less than an hour. Whereupon Washington made another appeal to the courage and manhood of his men; which proved so far successful, that a forlorn hope of forty finally screwed up pluck enough to follow him to the scene of danger. Moving with great caution and circumspection, and keeping all their ears and eyes about them, the party came at length to the spot mentioned by the scout; where, sure enough, they heard a somewhat scattering discharge of fire-arms, and divers outlandish noises, that bore, however, but a very slight resemblance to the terrific yells and whoops of Indian warriors. Advancing a few paces farther, a sudden turn of the road brought them in sight of two drunken soldiers, who were cursing and swearing and hallooing in a manner quite outrageous and immoral; and now and then, by way of adding a little spice to this part of their entertainment, firing off their pistols into the tree-tops. And this it was that had given rise to those wild rumors that had thrown the whole country into such a terrible panic. To this imprudent waste of breath and ammunition, the latter of which they had but little enough to spare, Washington put a rather sudden stop by ordering the lively young blades to be seized, and carried as prisoners to Winchester, where he kept them in severe confinement for more than a week after they had regained their sober senses. All this was ludicrous enough; and you may be sure that Washington, although grave and dignified beyond his years, had a hearty laugh over it the first time he found himself alone with one or two of his brother-officers.

In addition to his other cares, the duties of his office required him to visit, from time to time, the several forts along the frontier, to see that those already finished were kept in fighting order, and give directions for the proper construction of those still under way. Now, the little garrison of forty men, that Col. Dunbar had left to hold and defend Fort Cumberland against the combined armies of the French and Indians, was commanded by a certain Dagworthy, who, pluming himself upon the king's commission as captain, refused to own the authority and render obedience to the orders of Washington, who held only a governor's commission as colonel. It will be remembered, that Washington had a similar misunderstanding with Capt. Mackay, eighteen months before, at the Great Meadows, touching this same question of rank between royal and provincial officers, which had caused him great trouble and annoyance. Matters had now come to such a pass, that a little upstart captain of forty men could set at naught the authority of the commander-in-chief of the forces of a whole province, merely because he could boast a bit of paper embellished with the king's name. This was a degradation too grievous to be longer borne by a manly, independent spirit. Though sorely vexed and annoyed, Washington had too much self-respect and prudence to make a noise about the matter; but he inwardly resolved, that, as soon as the coming-on of winter would oblige the Indians to recross the mountains to the shelter of their homes beyond, he would take advantage of the breathing spell thus allowed him to make a journey to Boston, there to submit the question for final settlement to Gen. Shirley, who had succeeded Braddock to the chief command of all the British forces in America.

Accordingly, when the departure of the Indians brought the distressed inhabitants of the border the prospect of a few months' peace and quiet, he departed for Boston, in company with two of his brother-officers, Capts. Stewart and Mercer.

Now, in those days, a journey from the Old Dominion to the Bay City, a distance of but five hundred miles, in the depth of winter, when the roads were either deep and stiff with mire, or rough and knobby with frost, was really a greater undertaking than a voyage in a steamship from Boston to Constantinople would now be considered. Our young men travelled on horseback, as was the fashion of the day; and took with them their negro servants, who, riding behind with their masters' saddle-bags and portmanteaus, and dressed in fine livery, with gold lace on their fur hats, and blue cloaks, gave quite an air of style and consequence to the little cavalcade.

Washington's fame had long since gone before him, as was proved by the marked distinction and respect with which he was treated at Philadelphia, New York, and other places along the route. All were eager to behold with their own eyes the youthful hero, whose gallant conduct and wonderful escape at the defeat of Braddock had been so noised throughout the Colonies; and when we add to this his tall and commanding form, the manly beauty of his face, his dignified bearing, his rich and handsome dress, and the unequalled skill with which he managed his large and noble horse, we cannot wonder at the interest and admiration his appearance awakened in the minds of all who saw him.

When he got to Boston, where he likewise met with a flattering reception, he lost no time in making known to Gen. Shirley the business that had taken him thither. The justness and reasonableness of his complaints were promptly acknowledged by this officer, who, to place the vexed question beyond dispute, declared, that henceforward Capt. Dagworthy and all inferior officers, holding king's commissions, should own the authority and render obedience to the orders of all provincial officers of superior rank. This, the main object of his journey, thus happily disposed of, Col. Washington set out on his return to Virginia: but, knowing that the Indian war-whoop was not likely soon to be heard in the Shenandoah Valley, he indulged himself so far as to tarry two whole weeks at New-York City; and for the best of reasons, as I will tell you.

On his way to Boston, he had met here with the beautiful and accomplished Miss Phillipps, with whom he was vastly pleased; and it was for the nearer study of this young lady's charms, and further cultivation of her acquaintance, that our young Virginia colonel was now tempted for once in his life thus to linger on his way. Nothing came of it, however, that anybody now can tell; although the lady, you may stake your heads upon it, must and ought to have been highly flattered at being thus singled out by the young hero whose name and praise were in everybody's mouth. Perhaps his admiration never ripened into love; and, if it did, his modesty, as in the case of the Lowland Beauty, must have hindered him from making known his partiality. Whatever it may have been, it is, at this late day, of little consequence; for long before that year had passed away, with all its anxious cares, its perils and privations, and with all its train of ghastly Indian horrors, these tender sentiments had become to him nothing more than pleasant memories.

XIX.

DARK DAYS.

It were long to tell you, my dear children, all that happened to Washington, and all that he did for the next two or three years of his life. I shall, therefore, in as brief and clear a manner as may be, present to your minds a picture simply of those scenes in which he figured as the chief actor; although there were, it must be remembered, others who played a far more important part in this old French War than our young Virginia colonel.

The French and Indians, early in the spring of these years, were wont to cross the mountains at different points, and for months together follow their usual programme of fire, plunder, and massacre, till the approach of winter, when, loaded with booty and scalps, they would go as they had come, only to return on the opening of the following spring. With these cruel savages, and their scarcely less cruel white allies, neither age nor sex found mercy; old men, tender women, and helpless children, alike falling victims to their murderous tomahawks and scalping-knives. Farms were laid waste, crops destroyed, cattle butchered; and often, for days and nights together, the smoke could be seen in many directions at once, as it rose from burning barns and dwellings, and hung like a pall over the ill-fated land. At last, so great became the audacity of these pestilent savages, that they carried their depredations within cannon range of the very walls of Winchester; and, under their destroying hand, the rich and beautiful Valley of the Shenandoah seemed likely soon again to become a waste and desert place. It was a boast of theirs, that they could take any fort that could be fired; and round these places of refuge they would skulk and lurk with the greatest patience for a week at a time, quite content could they but get a single shot at such of the garrison as dared to show themselves beyond shelter of the walls. Sometimes, suddenly darting from their hiding-place, they would pounce upon little children playing in the woods, and, in full view of the fort, bear them away captives, never more to be seen by their bereaved parents, who could only listen in helpless anguish to the piteous cries of their little innocents, that grew fainter and fainter

The Farmer Boy and How He Became Commander-in-Chief

as their savage captors hurried them farther and farther into the gloomy depths of the wilderness.

Often, in their excursions along the frontier, Washington and his men would come upon the still smoking ruins of a happy home, or the hacked and mangled body of an unfortunate traveller who had been waylaid and murdered by the Indians in some lonely mountain glen. In after-life, the recollection of these harrowing scenes was to Washington so painful, that he could but seldom be brought to speak of them. Now and then, however, he would relate to a few friends some of these dark experiences; among which is the following, given in his own words, as a fair example of all the rest:—

"One day," said he, "as we were traversing a part of the frontier, we came upon a small log-house, standing in the centre of a little clearing, surrounded by woods on all sides. As we approached, we heard the report of a gun,—the usual signal of coming horror. Our party crept cautiously through the underwood, until we had approached near enough to see what we had already foreboded. A smoke was slowly making its way through the roof of the house; when, at the same time, a party of Indians came forth, laden with plunder,—consisting of clothes, household furniture, domestic utensils, and dripping scalps. We fired, and killed all but one, who tried to get away, but was soon overtaken and shot down. Upon entering the hut, there met us a sight, which, though we were familiar with scenes of blood and massacre, struck us—at least myself—with feelings more mournful than I had ever experienced before. On a bed, in one corner of the room, lay the body of a young woman, swimming in blood, with a gash in the forehead that almost separated the head into two parts. On her breast lay two little babes, less than a twelvemonth old, also with their heads cut open; their innocent blood, that had once flowed in one common vein, now mingling in the same current again. I was inured to scenes of bloodshed and misery; but this cut me to the heart; and never in my after-life did I raise my arm against a savage, without calling to mind the mother and her little twins with their heads cleft asunder. On examining the tracks of the Indians to see what other murders they might have committed, we found a little boy, and, a few steps forward, his father, both scalped, and both stone-dead. From the prints of the boy's feet, it seemed that he had been following the plough with his father, whom he had probably seen shot down; and, in attempting to escape, had been pursued, overtaken, and murdered. The ruin was complete: not one of the family had been spared. Such was the character of this miserable warfare. The wretched people of the frontier never went to rest without bidding each other farewell; for the chances were they might never wake again, or wake only to find their last sleep. When leaving one spot for the purpose of giving protection to another point of exposure, the scene was often such as I shall never forget. The women and children would cling around our knees, and mothers would hold up their little babes before our eyes, begging us to stay and protect them, and, for God's sake, not leave them to be butchered by the savages. A hundred times, I declare to Heaven, I would have laid down my life with pleasure under the tomahawk and scalping-knife, could I, by the sacrifice, have insured the safety of these suffering people."

The little folks can well imagine how scenes like these must have pained and wrung a heart like Washington's. But what could he do? His whole force did not exceed one thousand fighting men; with which he had to man more than twenty forts, and guard a frontier of nearly four hundred miles' extent. In addition to this, his men had been so scattered all the while at these different points, as to have placed it altogether beyond his power to give that attention to their military training which he had had so near at heart when he first entered upon his command. It naturally followed, then, that there was among the greater number an almost total want of order and discipline. They came and went when and where it suited their humor best; were impatient of control; wasted their ammunition, of which there was a great scarcity, in target-shooting; were far more ready to trouble their officers with good advice than aid them by prompt obedience to orders; and, if their sagacious counsels went unheeded, they would, without more ado, shoulder their rifles in high dudgeon, and tramp home. And, withal, so tender were they of what they were pleased to call their *honor*, that they would take it as quite an insult to be put on soldiers' rations; and were too proud or lazy—which with them was the same thing—to carry their own provisions while on the march; choosing, rather, to risk what chance might bring them, in the shape of bullocks, sheep, or pigs, which they would knock down, without a "By your leave" to the owner, and, after eating as much as satisfied their present hunger, would throw the rest away. Thus, between their wasteful defenders and their wasting invaders, the poor distressed inhabitants were brought to the verge of starvation.

The forts were too far apart to prevent the Indians from passing between; and the garrisons were too weak to lend each other aid when any of them chanced to be in hard, besetting need. This plan of giving defence to the border had been strongly opposed by Washington, who foresaw the disadvantages just hinted at, and had urged the exact contrary. This was, instead of having so many small forts, with but a handful of men in each, to fortify Winchester in the completest manner possible, with a view of making it the only stronghold and rallying-point of all the border, and to be manned by the main body of the troops, who were to give support to the smaller parties in their excursions against the enemy. Long before the war was ended, it was clearly to be seen, that, had this plan been adopted, much useless expenditure of money and shedding of blood would have been avoided. As it was, the cunning and watchful foe, whose motions were swift as the birds, and secret as death, could pass between these forts, not only unopposed, but even unobserved, and, without let or hinderance, lay waste the country for the protection of which they had been built. Under this most melancholy state of things, all the region west of the Blue Ridge was fast becoming the dreary and silent wilderness it had been in days gone by. Scarcely a shadow of its former population was left: some had fled to the forts for refuge; some had resettled in the eastern parts of the province; some had been carried away into cruel captivity; and many, very many, had met with a horrible death at the hands of the merciless invaders.

As if all this we have just related were not enough to try the patience and fortitude of young Washington, evil reports, injurious to his character, and charging him with being the author of all these failures and calamities, were set agoing by secret enemies at home. Foremost among these, you will be surprised and sorry to learn, was Gov. Dinwiddie, who had for some time past regarded with a jealous and envious eye this rising hope of the land, and was now seeking, by a variety of underhand means, to have him disgraced from the service, that Col. Innez, a particular chum of his, might be advanced to the chief command of the Virginia troops instead. The lower offices of the army he was zealous to bestow upon a knot of needy adventurers, who, being Scotchmen like himself, were in high favor with him, and scrupled not to make his likes and dislikes their own, if, by so doing, they could further their own private advantage. Perhaps Gov. Dinwiddie himself may not have been the direct author of these reports; but it is quite certain that his hungry hangers-on would never have dared whisper them had they not been fully aware of the ill-will he bore the person by whose injury they hoped to profit, and that they had but to do the thing, when their patron would not only wink at it, but even give it his secret approval.

When these malicious whisperings came to the ears of Washington, he was stung to the quick by such unfair and unmerited treatment. Feeling assured in his own conscience that he had done his whole duty as far as in him lay, all his strong and manly nature was roused to indignant anger, that his fair name should thus become the target of these arrows flying in the dark, without an opportunity being allowed him of a fair and open hearing in his own defence. He would have left the service at once,—the very end his enemies had been plotting so hard to bring about,—had not the frontier settlements, just at that moment, been threatened with more than usual peril; and to have deserted his post at such a time would have given his accusers real grounds for the charges, which heretofore had been but a mere pretence. Before the immediate danger was past that kept him at his post, many of his warmest and most influential friends, residing in different parts of the province, had written to him, earnestly entreating him not to think of resigning his command; assuring him, at the same time, that the base slanders of those evil-minded men had found no place whatever in the minds of his fellow-countrymen. On the contrary, beholding the courage, patience, and humanity with which he was discharging the high and sacred duties they had intrusted to him, they felt their love for him, and confidence in him, increasing every day. With this gratifying assurance that his conduct and motives were rightly understood by those whose approbation he was most desirous of winning, Washington now held on his course with renewed hope and spirit.

Thenceforward, Gov. Dinwiddie, as if to revenge himself for this failure of his base and selfish design, never let an opportunity slip of thwarting or annoying the man whose high public character his petty malice could not reach, and whose private worth his mean envy could not tarnish. His letters to Washington, the tone of which heretofore had been uncivil enough, now became harsh and insolent, full of fault-finding, and bristling all over with biting reproofs and unmanly insinuations. Although wretchedly ignorant of military matters, and at a distance from the seat of active operations, yet he must needs take upon himself the full control of all the troops of the province, without seeming to trouble his mind as to what might be the wishes and opinions of him who was in fact their true leader. Whether from a spiteful desire to perplex the object of his dislike, or natural fickleness of character, every letter from him brought with it some new plan. To-day, he ordered this; to-morrow, he ordered that; and, the next day, upset the other two by something quite different from either: so that Washington was often left completely in the dark as to what the uncertain meddler's wishes or plans really were.

At last, from being thus harassed in mind by these petty annoyances, and worn in body by the hardships of such rough service, his health failed him; and he was advised to repair to Mount Vernon, and there remain until his disease should take a more favorable turn. Here he lay for four long, weary months, before he could rejoin big regiment; during much of which time, his friends, who nursed and watched him, really regarded his recovery as doubtful. This is another instance of what so often seems to us a matter of wonder,—the power of a narrow-minded, mean-spirited, ill-tempered, false-hearted man to inflict pain on a noble and lofty nature.

A short time before the close of the war, it becoming quite certain that he had been putting public money, intrusted to his keeping, to private or dishonorable uses, Gov. Dinwiddie was recalled, and another sent over to fill his place. Being the man here described, and a petty tyrant withal, nobody was sorry to see him go, except the needy toadies who had hung about him, and who, seeing that nothing was likely to turn up for them in the New World, packed off to Scotland with their patron, as hungry and empty-handed as they came.

By the by, I must not forget to tell you of the heroic conduct of old Lord Fairfax. Greenway Court, as you no doubt remember, was in the Shenandoah Valley, not many miles from Winchester; and, situated on the very edge of a vast forest, was quite open to the inroads of the Indians, any one of whom, would have risked limb or life to get his bloody clutches on the gray scalp of so renowned a Long Knife. To meet this danger, as well as do his part towards the general defence, he mustered his hunters and negro servants, to the number of a hundred or thereabouts, and formed them at his own expense into a company of horse, with which the keen old foxhunter, now as daring a trooper, scoured the country from time to time, and did good service.

XX.

A NEW ENTERPRISE.

And thus these melancholy years came and went, with all their dark and painful experiences. A firm and self-reliant spirit like Washington's, however, could not be long cast down by even severer trials than those by which we have just seen his strength and manhood tested: so, from that time forward, come what might, he resolved to hold right on, nor bate a jot of heart or hope or zeal or patience, till the coming-on of better days, when, God willing, he might render a good and faithful account of this, his country's trust.

But the little folks must not suppose that Col. Washington and Gov. Dinwiddie were by any means the only persons of consequence who figured in this Old French War. On the contrary, there were others of far more importance at the time than they, not so much from any peculiar merit of their own, as from the part they played in those events; and upon whom, as such, I must needs bestow some passing notice, were it but to give to our story greater clearness and completeness. What concerns you to know of them at present I will briefly sum up in a few words, and make it as plain to you as a table of simple addition.

As Commander-in-chief of all the British forces in America, Braddock, as I have told you elsewhere, was succeeded by Gen. Shirley; who, proving himself unfit for the place, was soon recalled, and Lord Loudoun sent over from England instead; who, proving himself equally unfit, was dealt with in the same manner, and Gen. Abercrombie sent over instead; who also, proving himself incompetent, was also recalled, and Gen. Amherst sent over; who, proving a wiser choice, there followed happier results; and it fell to him, and to the brave young general, Wolfe, his next in rank, to bring this long and irksome war, in due course of time, to a glorious end. After the failure of Braddock's designs against Fort Duquesne, the conquest of Canada was made the chief object of the British Government; and the regions of the North thenceforth became the seat of war. While our young Virginia colonel, making the best use of the slender means allowed him, was struggling to keep back the pestilent savages and their pestilent white allies from his long line of frontier in the South and West, some of these leaders with their red allies, and some of the French leaders with their red allies, were, with various fortunes and misfortunes on either side, carrying on the war along the borders of the great Lake Ontario, the little Lakes Champlain and George, and up and down the mighty St. Lawrence.

Of these English leaders, I will mention Lord Loudoun merely, as being the only one with whom Washington had any special dealings. Had this nobleman come up to the hopes and expectations which many of the colonists were at first wild enough to entertain respecting him, he would have regained what Braddock had lost, overrun and conquered Canada, and made a clean finish of the whole French empire in America, in less than six months' time. They soon discovered, however, that he was one of those unlucky persons, who, knowing much, seldom know what use to make of their knowledge; who, having no will that they can call their own, can never turn the will of others to any good or seasonable purpose; and who, making a great show of doing, have never any thing to show in the end what they have done. In this last particular, Dr. Franklin, with that peculiar humor all his own, likened him to the picture of St. George on the sign, that was always on horseback, but never riding on.

Now, the recapture of Fort Duquesne, ever since the disgraceful failure of that first attempt, had been the one object nearest to Washington's heart. Foreseeing that there could never be peace or safety for the back settlements of the middle provinces so long as this stronghold of the enemy sent out its savage swarms to scourge and waste the border, he had repeatedly called Lord Loudoun's attention to the fact, and most earnestly urged its seizure as the only remedy. It was not, however, until early in the autumn of 1758, that an expedition, having for its object his long-cherished scheme, was set on foot. It was undertaken with a force of three thousand Pennsylvanians, twelve hundred North Carolinians, Washington's detachment of nineteen hundred Virginians, seven hundred Indians, and a few hundred regulars,—numbering in all seven thousand men, or thereabouts,—with Gen. Forbes for their chief commander.

The Farmer Boy and How He Became Commander-in-Chief

As an easy and rapid communication between the back settlements of Virginia and Pennsylvania would greatly lessen the difficulties of the coming campaign, this officer caused a road to be opened between Fort Cumberland and Raystown, a frontier post of the last-named province, where he had fixed his headquarters. Before the expedition could be put in motion, it was necessary that Col. Washington should go to Williamsburg to make known to the Virginia Legislature the needy condition of his soldiers, and make a call upon them for fresh supplies of tents, blankets, clothing, wagons, arms, &c.

Accordingly, attended by his trusty negro servant Bishop, and mounted on his splendid white charger,—both of which had been bequeathed to him by poor Braddock,—he set out on his journey, which proved an eventful one indeed to him, as you shall directly see. At the ferry of the Pamunkey, a branch of York River, he fell in with Mr. Chamberlin, an acquaintance of his, who, according to the hospitable customs of those good old times, invited him to call at his house, not far distant, and be his honored guest till morning. The young colonel would be only too happy to do so: but the nature of his business was such as would not admit of an hour's delay; indeed, it was quite out of the question, and he must hasten on. But, his friend repeating the invitation in a manner too earnest to be mistaken, he felt it would be uncourteous to refuse; and consented to stop and dine with him; on condition, however, that he should be allowed to proceed on his journey that same evening. At his friend's hospitable mansion he met with a gay and brilliant throng of ladies and gentlemen, who, though strangers to him, knew him well by reputation, and were but too proud to be thus unexpectedly thrown in his company. Among them was Mrs. Martha Custis, a young and beautiful widow of good family and large fortune. Her husband had died three years before; leaving her with two small children, a girl and a boy. She is said to have been a lady of most winning and engaging manners, and of an excellent and cultivated understanding. In stature she was a little below middle size, and of a round and extremely well-proportioned form; which, on this occasion, was set off to the best advantage by a dress of rich blue silk. Her hair was dark; her features were pleasing and regular; and there was a look of earnest, womanly softness in her hazel eyes, that found its way at once to the heart and confidence of all on whom it chanced to rest.

The little folks will not, I hope, suffer their admiration and respect for our young hero to be lessened in the least, if I tell them, that, like the rest of mankind who came within the magic circle of those bewitching charms, he was first surprised into admiration, and then led, whether or no, at a single step, into the enchanted realms of love. You have seen, how that, in his boyhood, he wrote broken-hearted verses to his Lowland Beauty; and how that, two or three years before, he had nearly yielded himself captive to the beautiful Miss Phillipps: which ought to prove to the satisfaction of all reasonable minds, that Washington, like other men, had a heart of real human flesh, that now and then gave him not a little trouble, despite that grave and dignified reserve which hung about him like a spell, and, even at that early age, was something to many quite overawing. The dinner, that had at first, in his hurry, seemed so long in coming on, seemed now quite as fast in going off. Not that I would have you suppose by this, that he thought the guests were showing any indecent haste to make way with the dishes that were set before them without number, and heaped up without measure, on Mr. Chamberlin's ample board. On the contrary, they partook of the good things of the table with a well-bred slowness, that would have been beyond his endurance to bear, had Mars been thundering with his iron fist at the gates of his fortress. But as it was Cupid, only tapping with his rosy knuckles at the casement of his heart, that dinner seemed no longer to him than, no, not half so long indeed as, the shortest snack he had ever eaten on horseback in the hurry of a forced march. The dinner over, Washington seemed in no haste to depart.

The trusty Bishop, knowing well what a punctual man his master always was, had appeared, according to orders, with the horses; and was plainly enough to be seen from the parlor window, had any one cared to look that way, patiently waiting with them in the pleasant shade of an apple-tree. The fiery white charger soon began to paw the ground, impatient at his master's unwonted tardiness; but no rider came. Bishop Braddock shifted his place once, twice, thrice, to keep himself and horses in the shade of the apple-tree; but still his master lingered: and the ivory grin that settled by degrees on his ebony mug showed that he had a sly suspicion of what was going on in the house. The afternoon sped away as if old Time, all of a sudden forgetting his rheumatism, had reached sunset at a single stride. Of course, they would not suffer him to depart at this late hour: so Bishop was ordered to restable the horses, and make himself easy and snug for the night with the colored folks down at their quarters. The next morning, the sun was hours on his journey to the west, before our love-smitten hero was on his way to Williamsburg.

Once in the saddle, however, all his yesterday's impatience returned upon him with redoubled force; and, giving his fiery white charger the spur, he dashed away at a break-neck speed on the road to the Virginia capital. It is said, so fast did he travel on that day, that, to keep up with him, Bishop Braddock ran serious risk of having his woolly nob shaken from his shoulders by the high, hard trotter he rode; and so sore was he made by the jolting he got, that, for a week thereafter, it was quite as much as he could do to bring his legs together. This last, by the way, is merely traditional, and must be received by the little folks with some caution.

Luckily, the White House, the residence of Mrs. Custis, was situated within a very few miles of Williamsburg; which gave young Washington many opportunities, during his two-weeks' stay at that place, of seeing her, and still further cultivating her acquaintance. Experience, that sage teacher who never spoke to him in vain, had taught him, that although there are many blessings of this world which seem to come of their own accord, yet there are a few that never come except at the asking for; and the chiefest of these is woman's love. So, resolving to profit by this knowledge, he did precisely what any wise and reasonable man would have done in his place,—overcame his troublesome bashfulness, and made the lady an offer of marriage; which she, precisely as any wise and reasonable woman would have done in her place, modestly accepted. The business that had called him to Williamsburg being at last disposed of, Washington took leave of his intended, after it had been agreed between them to keep up an interchange of letters until the close of the present campaign, when they were to be united in the holy bonds of wedlock.

The Farmer Boy and How He Became Commander-in-Chief

Upon his return to Winchester, he was dismayed to find that the English generals had taken it into their inexperienced heads to cut a new road from Raystown to Fort Duquesne by the way of Laurel Hill, instead of marching there at once by the old Braddock Road, as he naturally supposed had been their intention from the beginning. Foreseeing the consequences, he, in an earnest and forcible manner, hastened to represent to them the difficulties and disadvantages of such an undertaking. Cold weather would be setting in, he urged, long before they could cut their way through so many miles of that mountain wilderness to the point in question; and they would be obliged either to winter at Laurel Hill, or fall back upon the settlements until spring. This would give the enemy time to get full intelligence of their threatened danger, and send to Canada for re-enforcements. Their Indian allies too, as was their wont, would grow impatient at the long delay that must needs attend this plan if carried out; and, returning to their homes in disgust, would fail to render to the expedition their valuable services as scouts and spies, as had been expected of them. On the other hand, by taking the old road, they could march directly to the fort; which, being at that time but feebly garrisoned, must fall almost without a blow, and this, too, in less than half the time, and with less than half the trouble and expense. This prudent counsel, coming from one, who, from his knowledge of the country, had so good a right to give it, was nevertheless overruled. The English generals had gathered a most appalling idea of the difficulties and dangers of this route from the account Braddock had given of it in his letters. He had therein described it as lying through a region where the mountains were of the highest and steepest, the forests of the thickest and tallest, the rocks of the most huge and rugged, the swamps of the deepest, and the torrents of the swiftest. The route for the new road, on the contrary, according to the Pennsylvanians, who saw in it a great advantage to themselves, lay through a region where the mountains were not by far so lofty, the woods so thick, the rocks so huge, the swamps so deep, nor the streams so swift, or half so given to running rampant over their banks. All these advantages this route had, besides being fifty miles shorter. So, under the mistaken notion that more was to be gained by following a short road that would take them a long time in getting over, than by following a long one that would take them but a short time in getting over, they resolved to cut the new road.

This was a sore disappointment to Col. Washington; for he saw in it a likelihood of Braddock's folly being played all over again, and that, too, on a still larger scale. The tidings of glorious victories won by British arms in the North had filled the whole country with triumph and rejoicing, that rendered him all the more impatient at the tardiness with which their own expedition was moving forward. "He wished to rival the successes of the North by some brilliant blow in the South. Perhaps a desire for personal distinction in the eyes of the lady of his choice may have been at the bottom of his impatience." This last, it is but fair to say, is an assertion of our great countryman, Washington Irving; who, being a wise and learned historian, would not have made it, you may be sure, had not his deep insight into the workings of the human heart given him a perfect right so to do. If this be not enough to convince you that such was really the case, know that your Uncle Juvinell is entirely of the same opinion.

XXI.

MORE BLUNDERING.

At last, about the middle of September, the expedition was set in motion. Gen. Forbes sent Col. Boquet in advance, with nearly two thousand men, to open and level the road. In order to get more certain information touching the condition of the enemy,—his number, strength, and probable designs,—it was thought advisable by some of the officers to send out a large party of observation in the direction of Fort Duquesne. It was to be made up of British regulars, Scotch Highlanders, and Pennsylvania and Virginia rangers,—eight hundred picked men in all. Washington strongly disapproved the plan, on the ground that the regulars, being wholly unacquainted with the Indian mode of fighting, and unable to operate at so great a distance without taking with them a cumbrous train of baggage, would prove a hinderance, instead of a furtherance, to an enterprise which must needs owe its success to the caution, silence, secrecy, and swiftness on the part of those engaged. He therefore advised the sending-out of small companies of rangers and Indian hunters, who, knowing the country well, could spy out the enemy with less risk of detection to themselves, and, moving without baggage, could make far better speed with the tidings they may have gathered. The like advice, you may remember, he gave to Braddock. It met with a like reception, and the like disaster was the consequence.

The party set out from Laurel Hill, and began its tedious tramp across the fifty miles of wilderness that lay between that point and Fort Duquesne. It was headed by Major Grant, a noisy, blustering braggart, who, hankering after notoriety rather than seeking praise for duty well and faithfully done, went beyond the limits of his instructions; which were simply to find out all he could about the enemy, without suffering the enemy to find out more than he could help about himself, and, by all possible means, to avoid a battle. But, instead of conducting the expedition with silence and circumspection, he marched along in so open and boisterous a manner, as made it appear he meant to give the enemy timely notice of his coming, and bully him into an attack even while yet on the way. The French, keeping themselves well informed, by their spies, of his every movement, suffered him to approach almost to their very gates without molestation. When he got in the neighborhood of the fort, he posted himself on a hill overlooking it, and began throwing up intrenchments in full view of the garrison. As if all this were not imprudence enough, and as if bent on provoking the enemy to come out and give him battle on the instant, whether or no, he sent down a party of observation to spy out yet more narrowly the inside plan and defences of the fort; who were suffered not only to do this, but even to burn a house just outside the walls, and then return to their intrenchments, without a hostile sign betokening the unseen foe so silent yet watchful within.

Early the next morning, as if to give the enemy warning of the threatened danger, the drums of the regulars beat the *réveille*, and the bagpipes of the Highlanders woke the forest-echoes far and wide with their wild and shrilly din. All this time, not a gun had been fired from the fort. The deathly silence that reigned within was mistaken for fear, and made the fool-hardy Grant so audacious as to fancy that he had but to raise his finger, and the fort must fall. As Braddock's day had begun with martial parade and music, so likewise did this. As on that day the regulars were sent in advance, while the Virginians were left in the rear to guard the baggage, so was likewise done on this. On this day, as on that, not an enemy was to be seen, till, all of a sudden, a quick and heavy firing was opened upon them by Indians lurking in ambush on either side; while, at the same moment, the French flung open their gates, and, rushing out, mingled their loud shouts with the horrid yells of their savage allies. On this day, as had been done on that, the regulars, surprised, bewildered, panic-stricken, were thrown at once into disorder, and began firing their pieces at random, killing friend as well as foe. Unlike them, however, the Highlanders stood their ground like men, and, fighting bravely, cheered each other with their slogan, or wild battle-cry. On this day, as on that, the Virginians came up in the very nick of time to rescue the helpless regulars from utter destruction. On this, as on Braddock's day, the Indians, seeing the hopeless confusion into which the English had fallen, rushed out from their ambush with yells of triumph, and fell upon them, tomahawk and scalping-knife in hand. Major Lewis, the brave leader of the

Virginians, fought hand to hand with a tall warrior, whom he laid dead at his feet; but, soon overpowered by numbers, he was forced to surrender himself to a French officer, who received his sword. The blustering Grant, more lucky than the headstrong Braddock, saved his life by yielding himself up in like manner.

And now the rout became general, and the slaughter dreadful. Seeing the unlooked-for turn affairs had taken, Capt. Bullitt, whom Major Lewis had left to guard the baggage, gathered a few of his brave Virginians about him, and prepared to make a desperate stand. Sending back the strongest horses with the baggage, he blocked up the road with the wagons, and, behind the barricade thus formed, posted his men, to whom he gave a few brief orders how to act. These scanty preparations were hardly made, when the Indians, having finished the work of plunder, had sprung into swift pursuit, and were now close upon them, the wild woods ringing with their terrible whoops and yells. When they had come within short rifle-range, Capt. Bullitt and his men met them with a well-aimed volley of musketry from behind the shelter of their wagons; which, however, checked the savages but for a moment. Rallying on the instant, they were pressing forward in still greater numbers; when Capt. Bullitt held out a signal of surrender, and came out from behind the barricade at the head of his men, as if to lay down their arms: but no sooner were they within eight yards of the enemy, and near enough to see the fierce light that shone in their eyes, than they suddenly levelled their pieces, and poured a murderous fire into the thickest of them; then, charging bayonets, scattered them in every direction, and sent them yelling with astonishment and dismay. Before they could rally again, and renew the pursuit, Capt. Bullitt, having picked up many more of the fugitives, began a rapid but orderly retreat.

For several days thereafter, the fugitives, singly or in squads, came straggling into camp at Loyal Hannon. Of the eight hundred picked men who had been sent out with such good promise of success, twenty officers and two hundred and seventy-three privates had been left behind, either killed or taken prisoners. The whole force of the enemy, French and Indians, did not exceed that of the English: their loss in the battle is not known; but, as the Highlanders fought well and the Virginians fought well, it must have been heavy. The disaster foreboded by Washington had thus in reality fallen upon them. He was at Raystown when the dismal tidings came; and, although complimented by Gen. Forbes upon the bravery his rangers had displayed, was deeply grieved and mortified. In secret, many a man would have been gratified at beholding a prophecy he had uttered thus fulfilled; but Washington, incapable of such selfish and unnatural vanity, could but sorrow thereat, although it must needs increase his reputation for foresight and sagacity. As the only good thing that came from this defeat, I must tell you (and you will be glad to hear it) that Capt. Bullitt was rewarded with a major's commission for the gallant and soldierly conduct he had shown on that disastrous day in the midst of such fearful perils.

It was not until the middle of November that the whole army came up to Loyal Hannon, a little distance beyond Laurel Hill. Winter was coming on apace. What with rain and snow and frost, the roads would soon be rendered impassable, not only to wheeled carriages, but to pack-horses also. Fifty miles of unbroken wilderness lay between them and Fort Duquesne,—so long the goal of their hopes and toils, that seemed to recede as they advanced, like some enchanted castle we have read of before now in books of fairy tales, that poor benighted travellers never reach, although, in fancy, every step they take brings them nearer. The leaders began to talk seriously of going into winter-quarters at that place until the return of spring; and it seemed as if another of Washington's prophecies were likely to be fulfilled. But, about this time, two prisoners from Fort Duquesne were brought into camp; from whom they drew such an account of the weakness of the French, and the discontent and daily desertions of their Indian allies, as determined them to push forward without further delay, in spite of the wintry weather, and, at one fell blow, make a finish of the campaign. So, leaving behind them their tents and baggage, and taking with them but a few pieces of light artillery, they once more resumed their toilsome march. Col. Washington was ordered to go on in advance with a part of his detachment, to throw out scouts and scouting parties, who were to scour the woods in every direction, and thereby prevent the possibility of an ambuscade. This new arrangement, which showed that Gen. Forbes had the wisdom to profit by the folly of those who had gone before him, was a signal proof of the high esteem in which provincial troops were at last beginning to be held; and to which, by their courage, skill, and hardihood, they had, even years before, won so just a title.

When within a few miles of the French fort, the road began to show signs of the late disaster. Here and there were to be seen the blackened and mangled bodies of men, who, while fleeing for their lives, had been overtaken, and cut down by the murderous tomahawk; or, exhausted from the loss of blood, had there, by the lonely wayside, laid them down to die of their wounds. As they advanced, these ghastly tokens of defeat and massacre were to be met with at shorter and shorter intervals, till at length they lay thickly scattered about the ground.

Being now in close neighborhood with the enemy, the English moved with even greater caution and wariness than before; for they had every reason to suspect, that, as he had suffered them to come thus far without molestation, he meant to meet them here, under shelter of his stronghold, with a resistance all the move determined. When come in sight, however, what was their surprise, instead of beholding the high ramparts and strong walls, grim and frowning with cannon, which they had pictured to their minds, to find a heap of blackened and smoking ruins!

Deserted by his Indian allies, threatened with famine, cut off from all hope of aid from the North (where the English were everywhere gaining ground), and with a force of but five hundred men wherewith to defend the post against ten times that number, the French general had seen that the attempt to hold it would be but folly; and, like a prudent officer, had resolved to abandon it as his only chance of safety. Waiting, therefore, until the English were within a day's march of the place, he blew up the magazine, set fire to the works, and, embarking in his bateaux by the light of the flames, retreated down the Ohio.

Col. Washington, still leading the advance, was the first to enter; and, with his own hand planting the British banner on the still smouldering heaps, took formal possession thereof in the name of his Britannic majesty, King George the Second. And thus this stronghold of French power in the Ohio Valley, so long the pest and terror of the border, fell without a blow. Under the name of Fort Pitt, it was soon rebuilt, and garrisoned with two hundred of Washington's men; and, from that time to the war of the Revolution, it was held by the English, chiefly as a trading-post; and hence the dingy, smoky, noisy, thriving, fast young city of Pittsburg.

They now had leisure to pay the last sad duty to the dead who had fallen in the two defeats of Braddock and Grant. For three long years, the bodies of Braddock's slaughtered men had lain without Christian burial, bleaching in the sun of as many summers, and shrouded in the snows of as many winters. Mingled with the bones of oxen and horses, or half hidden in heaps of autumn leaves, they lay scattered about the stony hillsides,—a spectacle ghastly indeed, and most melancholy to behold. With many a sigh of pity for the hapless dead, and many a shudder of dark remembrance on the part of those who had been present at the scenes of rout and massacre, they gathered together the blackened corpses of Grant's men and the whitened bones of Braddock's men, and, digging a huge pit, buried them in one common grave. In this pious duty all took part alike, from the general down to the common soldier.

With the fall of Fort Duquesne, ended, as Washington had years ago foreseen, the troubles of the Western and Southern frontiers, and with it the power so long held by the French in the Ohio Valley. The Indians, with that fickleness of mind peculiar to savage races, now hastened to offer terms of amity and peace to the party whom the fortunes of war had left uppermost.

Having done his part, and so large a part, towards the restoration of quiet and security to his native province, the cherished object of his heart, for which he had so faithfully and manfully struggled, Washington resolved to bring his career as a soldier to a close. In his very soul, he was sick and weary of strife, and longed for peace. The scenes of violence and bloodshed had become loathing and painful to him beyond the power of words to tell; and, now that his country had no longer need of his services, he felt that he could, without reproach, retire to the tranquil shades of private life he loved so much, and had looked forward to with such earnest longings. He therefore, at the end of the year, gave up his commission, and left the service, followed by the admiration and affection of his soldiers, and the applause and gratitude of his fellow-countrymen.

With the fall of Quebec in the course of the following year (1759), this long and eventful Old French War was brought to a close, and French empire in America was at an end.

XXII.

WASHINGTON AT HOME.

Having done all that a brave and prudent man could for his country's welfare, Col. Washington now lost no time, you may depend upon it, in doing what every wise and prudent man should for his own: by which you are to understand, that on the sixth day of January, 1759, when he wanted but a few weeks of completing his twenty-seventh year, he was joined in the holy bonds of marriage with Mrs. Martha Custis, the blooming and lovely young widow, and mother of the two interesting little children,—to all of whom you had a slight introduction a short time ago.

The nuptials were celebrated at the White House, the home of the bride, in the presence of a goodly company of stately dames and fine old gentlemen, fair maidens and handsome youth,—the kith and kin and loving friends of the wedded pair. Had some belated traveller been overtaken by the little hours of that night, as he chanced to pass that way, he might have guessed, from the soft, warm light that shone from all of the many windows, and sounds of sweet music that came through the open doors, mingled with peals of joyous laughter, and the light tripping of numerous feet in the merry dance, that it must be a much-beloved and fortunate couple indeed that could draw together so happy and brilliant a throng under that hospitable roof. Had this same belated traveller wanted further proof of this, he had but to turn a little aside, and take a peep into the negro quarters, where he would have seen the colored folks in a jubilee over the grand occasion, and, to all appearances, quite as jolly as if the wedding had been an affair of their own getting-up, and in which each son and daughter of ebony had a personal interest. He would have seen them feasting on the abundant leavings that came down from the great house, till their faces shone again; and dancing to the music of Bishop Braddock's fiddle in a fashion all their own, and nobody's else.

First and foremost among these, with his wool combed the highest, his breeches the reddest, and manners the genteelest, might have

The Farmer Boy and How He Became Commander-in-Chief

been spied Black Jerry (who, when a negroling, had been saved from a thrashing by little George, as you well remember), showing off his heels to the envy of all male and the admiration of all female beholders. This last, it is but fair to say, is merely a fancy sketch of your Uncle Juvinell's, conjured up by recollections of certain long talks he often had, when a boy, with Black Jerry himself, at that time a very old negro of most excellent morals, who never failed, when his honored master's name was mentioned, to show his yellow ivory, and, for very respect, uncover his head, the wool of which was then as white as a Merino ram's.

This joyous event having passed thus happily off, Col. Washington, a short time after, repaired to Williamsburg to take his seat in the Virginia Legislature, or House of Burgesses as it was then called, to which he had been elected while absent on the last campaign; without, however, any particular desire or effort on his part, but by that of his numerous friends. Hardly had his name been enrolled as a member of that honorable body, when Mr. Robinson, Speaker of the House, by previous agreement arose and addressed him in a short but eloquent speech; thanking him, in the name of the rest, for the many and valuable services he had rendered his country during the past five years, and setting forth the gratitude and esteem with which he was regarded by his fellow-countrymen. Surprised out of his usual composure and self-possession by the honor thus unexpectedly done him, Washington, upon rising to thank the House, could only blush, stammer, and stand trembling, without the power to utter a single word. Seeing his painful embarrassment, Mr. Robinson hastened to his relief by saying with a courteous smile, "Sit down, Mr. Washington: your modesty equals your valor; and that surpasses the power of any language I possess." From that time till near the breaking-cut of the Revolution,—a period of fifteen years, he remained an active and influential member of this body; being returned from year to year by the united voice of the good people whose district he represented. Always thorough in whatever he undertook, he rested not until he had made himself muster of every point and question touching the duties of his new office; and, for method, promptness, prudence, and sagacity, soon proved himself quite as good a civilian as he had been a soldier.

The Farmer Boy and How He Became Commander-in-Chief

Early in the following spring, his first session ended, he betook himself to the sweet retirement of Mount Vernon; where, cheered by the company of his beautiful young wife and her interesting little children, he once more resumed those peaceful pursuits and innocent amusements to which he had looked forward with such bright anticipations amidst the perils and hardships of a soldier's life. War, as war, had already, young and ardent as he was, lost for him its charms; and he had learned to look upon it as a hard and terrible necessity, ever to be avoided, except in cases where the safety of his country should demand it as a last desperate remedy. Unlike most men of a bold and adventurous disposition, he all his life long took the greatest pleasure in the pursuits of a husbandman; and, to his manner of thinking, there was no lot or calling in life so happy, and none more honorable. Having now ample time for the indulgence of his tastes, he set about improving and beautifying his plantations, of which he had several, in the most approved style of that day. He planted orchards of various fruits; set his hillsides in grass; drained his marshes, and turned them into rich meadowlands; built mills and blacksmith-shops; enlarged his family mansion to a size better befitting his elegant and hospitable style of living; adorned the grounds about it with shrubbery, trees, and gardens; and converted the wild woods hard by into open and verdant parks. To his negro slaves he was the kindest of masters; ever mindful of their comfort, and extremely careful of them in sickness. Being of industrious habits himself, he would not make the least grain of allowance for sloth or idleness in them, or indeed in any one about him, but was strict in exacting of them the speedy and full performance of their allotted tasks; which, however, he always took care should come under rather than up to the measure of their strength. In his business habits, he was methodical to a nicety; kept his own books, and was his own overseer: for, having a strong aversion to being waited on, he never suffered others to do for him what he could do for himself. He kept a close and clear account, in writing, of the profits arising from the grain, tobacco, and other produce of his lands; and also the amount of his personal, household, and plantation expenses: by which means he could tell at a glance whether he were on the making or losing order, and readily detect whether any of whom he had dealings were given to careless or dishonest practices. So superior was the quality of every thing produced on his estate, and so widely known did he become for his honesty and uprightness in all business transactions, that, in time, a box of tobacco or a barrel of flour marked "George Washington, Mount Vernon, Va.," would be received into many foreign ports without the custom-house authorities opening or inspecting it.

He was an early riser. In winter, getting up before day, and lighting his own fire, he wrote or read two or three hours by candle-light. After a frugal breakfast of two small cups of tea and four small cakes of Indian meal, he mounted his horse, and rode about his plantations; seeing to every thing with his own eye, and often lending a helping hand. This duty done, he returned to the house at noon, and dined heartily, as well beseemed the active, robust man that he was, yet never exceeding the bounds of temperance and moderation both as to eating and drinking. His afternoons he usually devoted to the entertainment of his numerous guests, who thronged his hospitable mansion almost daily, and, if from a distance, abiding there for weeks together. After a supper frugal as his breakfast, if there was no company in the house, he would read aloud to his family from some instructive and entertaining book, or from the newspapers of the day; and then, at an early hour, retire to his room for the night.

Fish and game abounded in the woods and streams of his domain, as well as in those of the adjoining plantations; and he was thus enabled to indulge his fondness for angling and hunting to the utmost, whenever he felt so inclined. Two or three times a week, the shrill winding of the hunter's horn and the deep-mouthed baying of the fox-hounds would ring out on the clear morning air; when he might be seen at the head of a brilliant company of mounted hunters, dashing over the fields, across the streams, and through the woods, hot on the heels of some unlucky Reynard. I should not say unlucky, however; for although Washington was as bold and skilful a rider as could be found in thirteen provinces, and kept the finest of horses and finest of dogs, yet, for all that, he could seldom boast of any great success as a fox-hunter. But having the happy knack of making the best and most of every thing, be it toward or untoward, he always consoled himself with the reflection, that, if they had failed to catch their fox, they at least had their sport and a deal of healthful exercise; which, after all, should be the only object of fox-hunting. On such occasions, he was either joined by the neighboring gentry, or by such guests as chanced at the time to be enjoying the hospitalities of Mount Vernon. Among these, it was not unusual to find old Lord Fairfax, the friend and companion of his stripling days, who would come down from Greenway Court several times a year, with a long train of hunters and hounds, and by his presence double the mirth and cheer of all the country-side for miles and miles around. The fate of poor Reynard being duly settled, they would repair either to Mount Vernon, or to the residence of any one else of the party that chanced to be nearest, and wind up the sports of the day by a hunting-dinner, at which they were usually favored with the company of the ladies. At such times, Washington is said to have entered so keenly into the general hilarity, as to quite lay aside his accustomed gravity and reserve, and show himself almost as jovial as the merry old lord himself. Speaking of these amusements, brings to mind an anecdote of him, which I must tell you, as it will give you a still more lively idea of the promptness and decision with which he was wont to act whenever occasion demanded.

In those old-fashioned times, among many other laws that would seem odd enough to us at the present day, there were many very strict and severe ones for the protection of game, which made poaching (that is to say, hunting on private grounds without leave or license from the owner) no less a crime than theft, and punished the poacher as a thief accordingly. Now, there was a certain idle, worthless fellow, notorious for his desperate character, as being the most daring poacher in seven counties, who was known to be much in the habit of trespassing on the grounds belonging to Mount Vernon. This had been forbidden him by Washington, who had warned him of the consequences if he did not cease his depredations, and keep at a safe distance; but to this the sturdy vagrant gave little heed. He would cross over the river in a canoe, which he would hide, in some secret nook best known to himself, among the reeds and rushes that fringed the banks, and with his fowling-piece make ruinous havoc among the canvas-back ducks that flocked in great multitudes to the low marsh-lands of that region.

The Farmer Boy and How He Became Commander-in-Chief

One day, as Washington was going his accustomed rounds about the plantations, he heard the report of a gun in the neighborhood of the river; and, guessing what was in the wind, he forthwith spurred his horse in that direction, and, dashing through the bushes, came upon the culprit, just as he, paddle in hand, was pushing from the shore. The fellow, seeing his danger, cocked his gun, and, with a threatening look, levelled it directly at Washington, who, without heeding this in the least, rode into the water, and, seizing the canoe by the painter, dragged it ashore. Leaping then from his horse, he wrenched the fowling-piece from the astonished poacher, and fell to belaboring him in so clean and handsome a manner, as to make the unlucky wight heartily wish he had the wide Potomac between him and the terrible man whose iron grasp was then on his collar. My word for it, he never trespassed again on those forbidden grounds; and I dare be sworn, he never saw or ate or smelt a canvas-back thereafter, without feeling a lively smarting up and down under his jacket, and, it may be, his buckskin breeches too. It was not that a few dozen or even a hundred ducks had been shot on his premises, that Washington was thus moved to chastise this fellow; but that, in spite of wholesome warnings, he should go on breaking the laws of the land with such impunity; and also, that, instead of seeking to earn an honest livelihood by the labor of his hands, he should prefer rather to live in idleness, and gain a bare subsistence by such paltry and unlawful means.

Although verging on to middle age, Washington was still very fond of active and manly sports, such as tossing the bar and throwing the sledge, wrestling, running, and jumping; in all of which he had but few equals, and no superiors. Among other stories of his strength and agility, there is one which you may come across some day in the course of your reading, relating how that, at a leaping-match, he cleared twenty-two feet seven inches of dead level turf at a single bound.

Notwithstanding his modesty and reserve, he took much pleasure in society, and ever sought to keep up a free and social interchange of visits between his family and those of his neighbors. Besides their fine horses and elegant carriages, he, and others of the old Virginia gentry of that day whose plantations lay along the Potomac, kept their own barges or pleasure-boats, which were finished and fitted up in a sumptuous style, and were sometimes rowed by as many as six negro men, all in neat uniforms. In these, they, with their wives and children, would visit each other up and down the river; and often, after lengthening out their calls far into the night, would row home by the light of the moon, which, lending charms that the sun had not to the tranquil flow of the winding stream, and to the waving woods that crowned the banks on either hand, caused them often to linger, as loath to quit the enchanting scene. A few weeks of the winter months were usually spent by Mr. and Mrs. Washington either at Williamsburg or at Annapolis, then, as now, the capital of Maryland, where was to be found the best society of the provinces, and of which they were the pride and ornament. Here they entered into the gayeties of the season, such as dinners and balls, with much real relish; and, if the theatre added its attractions to the rest, Washington always made it a point to attend, as the entertainments there offered were of the sort that afforded him much delight. Nor was he loath to join in the dance; and your Uncle Juvinell, when a boy, had the rare fortune of meeting, now and then, with stately old dames, who had been belles in their days, and could boast of having had him for a partner; but, at the same time, they were wont to confess, that they were generally too much overawed by the gravity and dignity of his demeanor to feel entirely at their ease in his company, however flattered they may have been at the honor, which he, in his modesty, so little dreamed he was doing them.

Washington's marriage was never blessed with children; but he was all that a father could be to those of Mrs. Washington, whom he loved and cherished as tenderly as if they had been his own. As their guardian, he had the care of their education, and also the entire control of the immense fortune, amounting, in negroes, land, and money, to nearly two hundred thousand dollars, left them by their father, Mr. George Custis; and lovingly and faithfully did he discharge this sacred and delicate trust. Of these two children, the daughter (who was the younger of the two) died, in early maidenhood, of consumption. She had been of a slender constitution from her childhood; but, for all that, her death was an unexpected stroke, and was long and deeply mourned by Mrs. Washington and her husband. He is said to have been absent during her illness; but, returning a short time before she breathed her last, was so overcome with pity and tenderness upon seeing the sad change wrought in so brief a space by this dreadful disease in her fair young face and delicate form, that he threw himself upon his knees by her bedside, and, in a passionate burst of grief, poured out a fervent prayer for her recovery. The son now became the sole object of parental love and solicitude; and being, like his sister, of frail and uncertain health, was a source of much affectionate anxiety to his step-father as well as to his mother.

Both Mr. and Mrs. Washington were members of the Episcopal Church, and persons of the truest Christian piety. Every sabbath, when the roads and weather permitted, they attended divine worship either at Alexandria or at a church in their own neighborhood, and always took part in the religious exercises of the day with earnest and solemn devotion. In addition to the many charms of mind and person already mentioned, Mrs. Washington was a woman of great benevolence, and spent much of her time in acts of kindness and charity, which won her the love and gratitude of every poor family in the country around.

The Farmer Boy and How He Became Commander-in-Chief

Thus passed away fifteen tranquil years,—the white days of Washington's life. When we behold him as he was then, in the full strength and beauty of his ripened manhood, possessed of one of the handsomest fortunes in America, living in the bountiful and elegant style of those hospitable times, the pride and honor of his native province, the object of applause and gratitude to his fellow-countrymen, and of esteem and love to all whose privilege it was to call him friend; and, above all, blessed, in the partner of his choice, with a woman gifted with every grace and virtue that can adorn her sex,—when we behold him thus, well may we exclaim, "Verily, here was a man favored of Heaven in a special manner, and blessed beyond the lot of common mortals here below." But the clouds were gathering, and had long been gathering, that were soon to burst in storm and tempest over that happy and rising young land, and force him for many, many weary years from those, his loved retreats and peaceful pursuits, upon a wider, nobler field of action, wherein he was to play a part that should, in fine, win for him the name so dear to every American heart,—Father of his Country.

XXIII.

A FAMILY QUARREL.

"And now, Dannie, mend the fire with another Christmas log. You, Willie, open the windows at top and bottom, to let out the smoke the young historian will be sure to raise. Laura, my dear, trim the lamp; and you, Ella,—will you have the kindness to put a little sugar in your uncle's cider?—there's a darling! Ned, my boy, just tumble sleepy-headed Charlie there out of his comfortable nap, and touse him into his waking senses again. All right? Now I would have every one of you put your thinking-caps square and tight upon your heads, and keep all your ears about you; for, depend upon it, what I am now going to tell you is so full of hard points and tough knots, that, should you but lose the crossing of a 't,' or even the dotting of an 'i,' thereof, all the rest will be to you as so much hifalutin transcendentalism." (Here Uncle Juvinell took a gigantic swallow of cider, and pronounced the sugar a decided improvement; while the little folks wrote something on their slates, very long, and which no two of them spelt alike. Uncle Juvinell smacked his lips, and then resumed.)

Now, you must know, my dear children, that Great Britain, at the time of which we are speaking, was, and for many years had been, and, in fact, still is, and, in all human likelihood, will ever continue to be, burdened with a mountain-load of debt, which has already given her a frightful stoop in the shoulders, and may, in time, grow to such an enormous bulk as to break her sturdy old back outright. She had, as you have seen, added all French America to her dominions; but with this increase of power and glory, that made her king and nobles smile and sing with joy, came also an increase of debt and trouble, that made her common people scowl and growl with want and discontent. The expenses of the late war with France had added the weight of another Ætna or Sinai to the already staggering load that chafed her back; and, sorely grieved thereat, she began casting in her mind what might be done to lighten it a little.

The Farmer Boy and How He Became Commander-in-Chief

"My young Colonies," said our mother to herself, "which were planted by my love so many years ago, have grown to a goodly size, and prospered in a wonderful manner, under my fostering care, for which they owe me many thanks; and, being quite old and strong enough, must now repay it by taking their due share of my heavy burden."

Now, in all this, our mother did but deceive herself: for these Colonies had been planted by her oppression, not by her love; they had grown by her neglect, not by her fostering care. Therefore, they did not, as she pretended, owe her either love or thanks, although they gave her both; and she had no right to make them carry her burden without their consent. Strange as it may appear, these infant Colonies loved their mother to distraction, in spite of her unmotherly treatment of them; and would have gone any length to serve her,—even to the extent of bearing double the burden she would have laid on them,—had she been wise enough to consult their wishes about the matter, and suffer them to lay it on their own shoulders, in their own fashion, and of their own free will. To this the perverse old mother would not listen for a moment; and, without pausing to reflect what might be the consequences, took an Ætna or a Sinai from the load on her own shoulders, and clapped it on those of her children, who sat down under it plump, and sturdily refused to budge until they should be allowed to put it there themselves. Whereupon, this stiff-necked, wrong-headed old Britannia (for such was her Christian name) was exceeding wroth, made an outlandish noise among the nations, and even went so far (you will be shocked to hear) as to swear a little. Seeing there was no help for it but to remove this Ætna, she did so with as good a grace as could be expected in a family-quarrel; but was so indiscreet and short-sighted as still to leave a very small burden,—a mere hillock indeed,—just by way, as she said, of showing that she had the right to load and unload them when and how it suited her sovereign pleasure best.

Now, be it known, it was not the burden they had to carry of which these generous and high-spirited Colonies complained so bitterly; but that they should be denied the right of freely judging when and how and wherefore they were to be taxed,—a right that had been the pride and boast of Englishmen time out of mind. As for the matter of the burden, had that been all, they could have danced, ay, and blithely too, under Ætna and Sinai both, had the load but been of their own choosing, of their own putting-on, and of their own adjusting.

To add to their distress and humiliation, this hardest and unnaturalest of mothers now set over them judges, who were strangers to them, and loved them not; who were to hold their places, not, as theretofore, during good behavior, but at her will and pleasure. Another right, as dear to Englishmen as life itself, was taken from them,—to wit, the right of trial by jury; which gave every person, great or small, suspected or known to be guilty of any crime against the laws of the land, the privilege of a speedy trial, in open court, in the place where the crime may have been committed, and by a jury of honest and impartial men. Instead of this, the person accused was to be taken aboard some ship-of-war, likely as not a thousand miles from Christian land, and there tried by some authorities of the navy, who would know but little, and must needs care still less, concerning the person under trial, or his offence.

Under these and many other oppressions and injuries, the young Colonies groaned grievously. But, for all that, they were not to be subdued or broken. Time and again, they sent petitions to this unkindest and wilfulest of mothers, beseeching her, in humble and loving and dutiful terms, to remove this degrading burden from their shoulders, and once more receive them as children into her maternal bosom; warning her, at the same time, of what must be the melancholy consequences, if she hearkened not to their prayers. Then was the time, if ever, when, by a few kind words betokening a desire for reconciliation, she might have secured and made fast the love of these devoted and affectionate children for ever; and, had she been as wise as she was powerful, even so would she have done. But, like the Egypt of olden times, she did but harden her heart against them all the more, even to the hardness of the nether millstone; and only sought how she could the more easily grind them into obedience and submission. She had grown to be mighty among the nations, this Britannia. Her armed legions told of her power by land; her ships of war and her ships of commerce whitened a hundred seas. The great sun, that set on every kingdom of the known earth, she boasted never went down on her dominion. Wherefore was she swollen and big with pride, and from a high place looked haughtily down upon the little nations at her feet. What height of presumption was it, then, in these insignificant young Colonies, struggling for bare existence off there on the uttermost edges of the civilized earth, thus to lift themselves against her sovereign will, and dare dispute her high decrees! It was not to be borne: she would humble them for this presumption, chastise them for their disobedience, and show them what a terrible thing it was to provoke her wrath. Her heart thus steeled to mercy, she stayed not her hand, but sent her hosts of armed men in her fleets of armed ships, to lay her heavy yoke, and fit it firm and fast on the necks of her rebellious children.

Beholding this, and that it were vain to hope for reconciliation, the Colonies, with one voice, with one indignant voice, exclaimed, "Now, since our mother seems bent on treating us as slaves and strangers, and not as children, then are we compelled, in our own defence, to treat her, not as our mother, but as a stranger and our enemy. And bear us witness, O ye nations! how long and humbly and earnestly we have prayed that there should be love and peace between us and this our mother; and bear us witness also, that, although we now lift our rebellious hand against her, there is no hatred in our hearts, even now, but rather sorrow unspeakable, that she should at last have driven us to this saddest, this direfulest of alternatives." Then, moved with one spirit (that of the love of freedom), and bent on one purpose (that of the defence of their sacred rights), they rose in their young strength, and, commending their just cause to the God of hosts, made that last appeal,—which, to a brave and virtuous people, has ever been the last,—the appeal to arms. And so they did, while the nations looked on in wonder and applause.

XXIV.

THE CAUSE OF THE QUARREL.

But, my children, I must tell you, in other and perhaps plainer words, what these measures were that led to such momentous results, why resorted to, how carried out, and by whom.

From what you have just been told, you can have no difficulty in guessing that Great Britain was desperately in debt, and in the very mood to resort to desperate measures of delivering herself therefrom. Her being in this particular mood at that particular time (for it is only now and then that she has shown herself so unamiable) was owing chiefly to the fact, that she was just then under the rule, or rather misrule, of that narrow-minded, short-sighted, hard-fisted, wrong-headed man, who commonly goes in history by the name of King George the Third. Had he been the superintendent of a town workhouse, he might perhaps have acquitted himself respectably enough; or, if I may be so bold, he might have served a life-term as Governor of London Tower, and gone to his grave without any great discredit or reproach: but, in all human reason and justice, he certainly had no more business on the throne of England than your Uncle Juvinell himself. His ministers, who were of his own choosing, were vultures, of the same harsh, unsightly plumage, and, at his beck or nod, stood ready to do whatever knave's work he might have on hand,—even to the grinding of his people's bones to make his bread, should his royal appetite turn that way.

With such men at the helm of State, it is no wonder, then, that unwise and oppressive measures should be resorted to for raising money, or, as it is more properly called in such cases, a revenue, for paying the debts and keeping up the expenses of the government. The first pounce they made was on their young Colonies in America, whom they sought to burden with heavy taxes laid on exports, or articles of commerce sent out of the country, and on imports, or articles of commerce brought into the country. The principal articles thus taxed were paper, painters' colors, glass, sugar and molasses, and tea. The tax-money or revenue scraped together from the sale of these articles—and which made them dearer to him who bought and him who sold, according to the amount of duty laid on—was to be gathered into the public treasury for the purposes aforesaid. Another plan for raising revenue, hit upon by these ingenious kites, was that famous one called the "Stamp Act," the design of which was to compel the people of the Colonies, in order to make their business transactions good and valid, to use a certain kind of paper, having on it a certain stamp. Each kind of paper had its own particular stamp, and could only be applied to a certain purpose specified thereon. Thus there was a deed stamp-paper, the will stamp-paper, the note-of-hand and bill-of-exchange stamp-paper, the marriage stamp-paper; and, in short, stamp-paper for every concern in life requiring an instrument of writing. The paper itself was altogether a commodity of the government, by whom it was manufactured, and sold at prices varying from a few pence up to many pounds sterling of good, hard English money, just according to the magnitude or nature of the business in hand. Had it gone into effect, it must needs have borne on the dead as well as on the living: for, if the last will and testament of a deceased and lamented relative were not written on paper with the proper stamp, it could not have been good and valid in the king's eyes; and this would have led to grievous misunderstandings between the bereaved and affectionate heirs, and perhaps the deceased himself, in consequence, would have slept uneasily in his grave.

Another oppressive measure—the design whereof, however, was for saving money, rather than for raising revenue—was that of quartering troops upon the country in time of peace; by which means they must needs be supported to a great extent by the people so sponged upon.

But the most brilliant stroke of all was an act forbidding the Colonies from trading with any foreign ports, and from manufacturing certain articles, lest the value and sale of the same articles manufactured in England, and to be sold in America, might be lowered or hindered thereby.

I have already mentioned, how that the right of choosing their judges and other civil officers, and the right of trial by jury, had been taken from them,—measures that had a meanness and odium quite their own; as serving no end of profit, but merely as safety-valves, through which the royal bile might find vent now and then.

Now, the good people of the Colonies, as I have hinted elsewhere, would not have raised the hue and outcry that they did against these measures, had it not been for one thing, which to them, as Englishmen, was all in all; to wit, the right of taxing themselves, and legislating or making laws for themselves through persons of their own choosing, called representatives. And this is, my little folks, what is meant by taxation, and legislation by representation, in a nation. You will do well to bear this in mind continually; for it is the very keystone to the arch of all true government.

This right of representation, however, was denied them; for what earthly reason, no one, not in the secret, could imagine. As the king himself was never able to render a reason for any thing he did, his ministers would not for any thing they did, and the parliament dared not for any thing they did.

What could they do, then, but send petitions to the king, and remonstrances to the parliament, complaining of, and crying out against, their many grievances, and deploring and demanding that they be removed and redressed. Although they did this with more dignity and respectfulness, with more clearness and ability, than the like thing had ever been done before, or has been since, by any people, yet their petitions were spurned by the king, because they were just and manly, and he was not; and their remonstrances went unheeded by the parliament, because they were wise and reasonable, and it was not.

Failing to get redress for their grievances, the colonists resolved that the source of these same grievances should not be a source of profit to those who imposed them. To bring about this result, they, as one man, entered into what was called the "non-importation agreement,"—or, in other words, an agreement by which they solemnly pledged themselves to abstain from the use of all articles burdened with a tax, until such tax should be removed; and, furthermore, that they would not buy or use any thing that they were forbidden to manufacture themselves; and, still furthermore, that not a ship of theirs should trade with British ports, until the act forbidding them to trade with foreign ports should be repealed. Some of them, I dare say, would have gone so far, had that been possible, as to pledge themselves not to die, until the Stamp Act, compelling them to write their wills on stamp-paper, was also repealed. This agreement was so rigidly observed, that the men took to wearing jeans, and the women linsey-woolseys, which they wove in their own looms; the old ladies drank sassafras-tea, sweetened with maple-sugar; and old gentlemen wrote no wills, but declared them on their death-bed to their weeping families by word of mouth. Whether the people stopped marrying or not, it is not known with certainty; but from my knowledge of human nature, which is extensive, I do not think I should greatly hazard my reputation as a historian, were I to state flatly, roundly, and emphatically, that it had not the least effect in that way.

The days on which these measures were to go into effect were observed by the colonists as days of fasting, prayer, and humiliation. All business was laid aside, the shops were closed, the churches opened, and the church-bells tolled as on some funeral occasion; and between praying at church, and fasting at home, and brooding over their grievances, the good people were very miserable indeed. Although they suffered great inconvenience from their observance of the non-importation agreement, yet they bore it patiently and cheerfully, like men who felt that their cause was just and right. But the sudden stoppage of the immense trade that flowed from the colonial ports into those of the mother-country told dreadfully on the commerce of Great Britain; and British merchants and British manufacturers, and British people in general, soon began to suffer even more than the colonists themselves. Whereupon, a counter stream of petitions and remonstrances set in upon the king and parliament from the people at home, who declared that the country would be ruined, if these odious measures, crippling American commerce, were not speedily withdrawn. Said they, "If we cannot sell the Americans our broadcloths, our flannels, and our silks, the obstinate men of that country will stick to their jeans, and the perverse women to their linsey-woolseys, till we are undone for ever. In that one pestilent little town of Boston, our trade in silks alone is not so good by fifty thousand dollars a year as it has been heretofore: and we humbly entreat that our American brothers be allowed to trade with us and foreign nations as in days gone by; for you must see by this time with your own eyes, that we, as a nation, are growing poorer every day under this state of things, instead of richer every year as had been expected."

The commissioners—that is to say, the persons who had been appointed by the British Government to bring or receive the stamp-paper, and give it circulation throughout the Colonies—were mobbed and pelted by the indignant people, whenever and wherever they made the least attempt to do their odious work. In consequence of this determined opposition, the paper never went into circulation: so it was stocked away in outhouses, and there left to mould and to be eaten by rats and mice, if their stomachs were not too dainty for such vile provender. Thus this famous piece of ingenuity, the Stamp Act, had no other effect than that of giving the civilized world a hearty laugh, and increasing the British debt just so much as the paper cost, instead of lessening it, as its inventors, in their blind confidence, had hoped.

Beholding how utterly had failed all their pet schemes for raising revenue, the narrow-minded king, and the king-minded ministry, and the many-minded parliament, were, so to speak, thrown on their haunches, and forced to eat their own folly; which, I dare say, they found less palatable than their roast beef and plum-pudding. In other words, they repealed the Stamp Act; with one stroke of the royal pen, struck off the taxes laid on the above-mentioned articles; and once more gave the Colonies full liberty to manufacture whatsoever, and re-open commercial intercourse with whomsoever, they chose. And thus this non-importation agreement worked like a charm: it brought about in a trice what petitions and remonstrances had failed to accomplish in years.

When tidings came of what had been done at home, there was great rejoicing throughout the provinces: the church-bells were tolled to another tune than that with which they had been tolled a short time before; the good people met at church, but this time to give thanks; and went home, not to fast, but to feast; and were now quite as comfortable as they had before been miserable. But I have gone a little too far, however. There was one circumstance that greatly dampened the general feeling of joy, and made a mere thanksgiving of what might else have been a high-sounding jubilee. This was the tax on tea, which had not been struck off along with the rest, but had been suffered to remain; not that any great revenue was expected to arise therefrom, but simply to show that they—the king and parliament—had not disclaimed or yielded up the right to tax and burden the Colonies when and how they thought fit and proper. This vexed the American people sorely; for though the bulk of the nuisance had been taken away, yet all the odor still remained: or, speaking more plainly, the right of laying such burdens on themselves, of their own free will, was still denied them; and this, in fact, was the very thing that made it so intolerable for them to bear. "Is it," said Washington in a letter to a friend, "the duty of threepence per pound upon tea that we object to as burdensome? No; but it is the right to lay this duty upon ourselves for which we contend."

Therefore, as far as the commodity tea was concerned, the people of the Colonies still observed the non-importation agreement. From some of the ports, the ships that had come over from England laden with this delightful plant were sent back, without being suffered to discharge their cargoes; in others, where it had been landed, it was not allowed to be sold, but was stowed away in cellars and the like out-of-the-way places, where it moulded, or became the food of rats and mice, whose bowels, if we may trust the testimony of some of our great-grandmothers, were so bound up thereby, that a terrible mortality set in among them, that swept them away by cart-loads.

Now, the East-India Company, to whom had been granted the sole privilege of trading in tea for the space of a hundred years, if I remember rightly, were greatly alarmed at the consequences of the tea-tax. Enormous quantities of the article had begun to accumulate in their London warehouses, now that there was no market for it in America, which hitherto had fed the purse in their left-hand pocket, as did that in Great Britain the larger one in their right-hand pocket. "Something must be done," said they to themselves (they certainly said it to nobody else),—"something must be done, or these high-spirited women of America will drink their wishy-washy sassafras

The Farmer Boy and How He Became Commander-in-Chief

till their blood be no thicker than whey, and the purse in our left-hand pocket become as light and lean and lank as when we sent our first ship-load thither years ago." This "something to be done" was a loud petition to parliament, praying for speedy relief from the ruin, which has an uncomfortable fashion of staring at great mercantile companies, and was now staring them full in the face.

So, putting their heads together, the king and parliament hit upon an ingenious plan, by which they, the East-India Company, could sell their tea, and the government collect the duty thereon. It was this: The price of the article should be so far reduced, that it would be lower, even with the duty on it, than, at the usual rate of sale, without any duty at all. This was a brilliant scheme indeed, and would have succeeded to admiration, had the good people of America been a nation of bats and geese; but, as they were not, the scheme failed disgracefully, as you shall presently see.

By way of giving this plan a trial, a few ships loaded with tea were sent over to Boston, where they lay for some time in the harbor, without being permitted by the people to land their cargoes. One day, as if to show the king and ministers and parliament, the East-India Company, and the whole British nation, that they, the Americans, were, and had been from the very beginning, desperately in earnest in all that they had said and done for years past, a party, composed of about fifty of the most sober and respectable citizens of Boston and the country around, disguised themselves as Indians, and went aboard these ships. Not a word was to be heard among them; but, keeping a grim and ominous silence, they ranged the vessel from stem to stern, ransacked their cargoes, broke open the tea-chests, and, pouring their contents into the sea, made the fishes a dish of tea, which is said to have had the same effect on them as on the rats and mice. This done with perfect coolness and sobriety, the party returned to their homes as orderly and silent as they had come; not the first movement towards a mob or tumult having been made by the people during the whole proceeding.

This affair, commonly known in history as the Boston Tea-party, and which took place in 1774, overwhelmed his majesty with stupid astonishment, threw his ministers into fits of foaming rage, fell like a thunder-clap upon the House of Parliament, and effectually demolished the last forlorn hope of the East-India Company. The spirit of resistance on the part of the Colonies had now been carried to such a length, that the home-government determined to send over the military to awe them by the terror of its presence into obedience to their unreasonable and oppressive demands; and, should not this be found sufficient, to compel them into submission by the force of its arms.

Oh, woful, woful, that ever a tyrant should live to keep his dragon-watch on the birth of the free-born thought, the independent wish, and ere the full, clear light of heaven descend upon it, warming it into strength and beauty, to seize and crush it into slavish fear, and love and justice without power to stay his impious hand!

XXV.

RESISTANCE TO TYRANNY.

With what deep and earnest interest Washington watched the course of these momentous events may be readily imagined, if we reflect how much of his life had been already spent in the service of the public, and how near he had ever kept the good and welfare of his native land at heart.

He was not a mere looker-on, but one of those who had in the very beginning shown themselves ready to enter, heart and hand and fortune, into all just and lawful measures of resistance to oppression in every shape and form; but, with his usual modesty, forbearing to push himself forward, which served, no doubt, to add to his example still greater weight and influence, and make it all the more illustrious. He rigidly observed the non-importation agreement, and was, in fact, one of the first to propose its adoption; and none of the articles therein named were to be seen in his house until the odious burdens laid thereon had been removed.

Little or no lasting good, however, could be expected from these, or indeed any measures, unless the Colonies should come to a clearer and fuller understanding, one with another, touching the troubles that concerned all equally and alike. To bring this much-to-be-wished-for end about, it was resolved that a general assembly of all the Colonies should be called, wherein each province, through its representatives chosen by the people thereof, should have a voice. As the first step towards this object, conventions were summoned in the various provinces, the members whereof had the authority to choose from among their number those who were to be their representatives or mouth-pieces in this great Colonial Assembly, since known in history as the Old Continental Congress.

Patrick Henry (the great American orator), Mr. Pendleton, and Washington were those appointed to represent Virginia. Accordingly, about the middle of September, 1774, these three Congress-men set out together on horseback for Philadelphia, the

The Farmer Boy and How He Became Commander-in-Chief

place of meeting. Arrived here, Washington found assembled the first talent, wisdom, and virtue of the land. It was to him a sublime spectacle indeed,—that of the people of many widely separated provinces thus met together to give voice and expression to what they felt to be their sacred rights as freemen and free Englishmen. To add still greater solemnity to their proceedings, and give their cause the stamp of the just and righteous cause they felt it to be, it was resolved to open the business of each day with prayer. Next morning, there came a report that Boston had been cannonaded by the king's troops, who had been stationed there for many weeks past. Although this afterwards turned out to be false, yet, at the time, it had a most beneficial effect, in drawing still nearer together those who but the day before had met as strangers, by impressing their minds with a still deeper sense of the sacredness of the trust imposed on them by their country, and by bringing more directly home to them their common danger, and dependence one upon another. The minister, before offering up his prayer, took up the Bible to read a passage therefrom, and, as if providentially, opened at the thirty-fifth Psalm, which seemed to have been written expressly for this great occasion, and began thus: "Plead my cause, O Lord, with them that strive with me; fight against them that fight against me." What wonder, then, that, under circumstances like these, they should feel their hearts joined together in stronger, holier bonds of union, as they knelt side by side on that memorable morning, commending their just cause to the Ruler of nations? For several minutes after they had resumed their seats, a profound and solemn silence reigned throughout the house; each looking the other in the face, as if uncertain how to set about the great work that had brought them together, and no one willing to open the Assembly. The silence was becoming painful and embarrassing; when Patrick Henry at length arose, and began addressing the House, at first in a faltering voice and hesitating manner, which soon, however, as he warmed with his subject, gave place to a bolder, higher strain, till, long before he had ended, the hearts of his hearers were thrilled with a flow of eloquence, the like of which none present had ever heard before; and, when it ceased, each felt that he had just been listening to the greatest orator, not of Virginia only, but of all America. The burden of his declamation was the oppressive and unlawful system of taxation devised by Great Britain against her American Colonies; the severe restriction laid on their commerce; the abolition of the right of trial by jury, and of choosing their own judges; the danger that must ever threaten their liberties, if they suffered troops of war to be quartered upon them in times of peace; and, above all, that they should be denied the right of taxing themselves, of making their own laws, and of regulating their internal concerns, as seemed to their judgment wise and proper, through representatives of their own choosing. To get redress for these and similar grievances, was the chief, and, I may say, the only object for which this first Congress had been called; for at that time, and for a long time after, no one harbored such a thought as that of breaking with the mother-country, with a view of achieving their independence. To this end, they now applied themselves with deep and sober earnestness, and brought to their work all the resources that their wisdom and experience could command.

The first session of the Old Continental Congress lasted fifty-one days. Such was the decorum with which they conducted their proceedings, such the eloquence, force, and precision with which they set forth their grievances, such the temperate and dignified tone that marked their petitions to the king, and such the manliness, firmness, and unwavering constancy with which they persisted in battling for their right as freemen to be represented in the councils of the nation, that thousands of their brothers across the Atlantic were filled with wonder and admiration. And here, for once and for all, be it known to you, my dear children, and, in justice to the British nation as a people, never fail hereafter to bear it in mind, that there were many, very many, perhaps a large majority, of our English uncles, who deeply sympathized with our fathers in their troubles, and heartily condemned the oppressive burdens heaped upon them by the king and his ministers. Even in the House of Parliament itself were there many of the greatest spirits of that age, who had all along opposed these harsh and unjust measures of the government towards the Colonies, and were now so impressed with all that marked the proceedings of this first Colonial Congress, that they exerted themselves in behalf of their oppressed brothers in America with more zeal than ever before, and pleaded their cause in strains of eloquence that shall ring in our ears, and dwell in our hearts, till history shall tell us we have ceased to be a nation.

And well indeed they might admire and praise; for what with the eloquence of such men as Henry and Rutledge, the learning of such men as Hancock and Adams, the wisdom of such men as Washington, and the pure and exalted character of them all, it was a body of men, the like of which had never before assembled together in any age or country.

Patrick Henry, upon being asked who was the greatest man in the Congress, replied, "If you speak of eloquence, Mr. Rutledge, of South Carolina, is by far the greatest orator; but, if you speak of solid information and sound judgment, Col. Washington is, beyond all question, the greatest man on that floor." Had Mr. Rutledge been asked the same question, he would as readily have pronounced Patrick Henry the greatest orator, as indeed he was.

Bent on one common object, encompassed by dangers that threatened all alike, and glowing with the same ardent and heroic spirit, they seemed for the time to have quite forgotten that they were the natives and representatives of many different and widely separated provinces, and to think that they were, as Patrick Henry happily expressed it, not Carolinians, not Pennsylvanians, not Virginians, so much as that they were Americans; and had been sent there, not so much to represent the will and wishes of the people of their respective provinces, as of those of the whole American people. Thus Union became the watchword throughout the Colonies. And by union alone were they able to make a stand against tyranny; by it alone came off victorious in the end; by it alone won for themselves a place among the nations; and by it alone can their posterity hope to hold that place as a powerful, free, and happy people.

Having done all that could be done for the present, the Congress was adjourned, and the members returned to their homes to await the result of the petitions and remonstrances they had sent on to the king and parliament. Although these were couched in moderate and respectful terms, expressing their unaltered attachment to the king and his family, deploring that there should be aught but peace and good-will between them, and entreating him not to drive his children to the dreadful alternative of taking up arms in their defence, yet, like those that had gone before them, they were received with contempt or indifference, and failed to awaken in the king's mind any sentiment of mercy, or desire on the part of the parliament for reconciliation with their younger brothers in America. Here was the last, the golden opportunity, wherein, by an act of simple justice, by an expression of Christian kindness, they might have won back to obedience and love this much-injured people; but under the mistaken and fatal belief that they were all-powerful, and that, if they yielded up these pretended rights, the colonists would never rest until they had thrown off and trampled under foot all authority, they suffered it to pass unheeded, lost for ever.

A short time after the adjournment of Congress, at a second Virginia Convention, held at Richmond, Patrick Henry, in closing one of the grandest efforts he ever made, thus boldly declared his mind: "The time of reconciliation is past; the time for action is at hand. It is useless to send further petitions to the government, or to await the result of those already addressed to the throne. We must fight, Mr. Speaker: I repeat it, sir, we must fight! An appeal to arms and to the God of hosts is all that is left us!" The great orator did but give voice to the feelings and sentiments of thousands of pure patriots, among whom was Washington, who represented his district in this convention also. No one regretted more sincerely than he that they were thus compelled to take up the sword as the only remedy of their wrongs and grievances. In his own mind, he had fully resolved, if needful, to devote his life and fortune to the cause; and was willing, he told his brother, to arm and equip a thousand men at his own expense, and lead them to the succor of Boston, at that time blockaded by the British fleet. Grave and thoughtful, and pondering deeply all these things, he went to his home; and, in this frame of mind, the winter months passed slowly by.

It was now apparent to all, that open hostilities between the Colonies and the mother-country were no longer avoidable; and on the nineteenth of April, 1775, the battle of Lexington announced to the world that the first blood of a desperate struggle had been shed, and that civil war, with all its train of horrors, had begun.

The Farmer Boy and How He Became Commander-in-Chief

When the tidings reached Mount Vernon, the impressions made on Washington's mind were solemn and profound, if we may judge from a letter written at the time, in which he says, "Unhappy it is to reflect, that a brother's sword has been sheathed in a brother's breast, and that the once-peaceful plains of America are to be drenched with blood, or inhabited by slaves. Sad alternative! But can a virtuous man hesitate in his choice?" Early in May, as he was just on the eve of setting out for Philadelphia to take his seat in the second session of the Congress, news reached him of the capture of Ticonderoga by Col. Ethan Allen. It was a brilliant little exploit enough, and the very kind to raise undue expectations in the many, who looked no further into the future than to-night, when it is yet evening; but it could have no other effect than to deepen the thoughtfulness of a mind like Washington's, that could look through the glare of these accidental hits of war, and behold the untried perils still further beyond.

As the war had now begun in earnest, so dreaded and deeply deplored by all the good men, as the only remedy left to their distress, the deliberations of the second Congress turned chiefly on the devising of means for their defence and safety. Towards this object, nothing effectual could be done till some person was fixed upon to be the leader of the army, which they had yet, in large measure, to raise, arm, and equip.

There were not a few, who, for age, talent, experience, fortune, and social position, as well as for the sacrifices they had already made to the cause, were, in the opinion of their friends, and perhaps in that of their own, justly entitled to this high distinction. After some time spent in viewing the matter in all its bearings, and carefully weighing the claims of each, without being able to fix upon a choice, John Adams decided the question by addressing the House to the following effect: That the person intrusted with a place of such importance to Americans must be a native-born American; a man of large fortune, in order to give him a strong personal interest in the issue of the contest, and the means of carrying it on; he should be a man of military experience, and accustomed to the government of large bodies of men; he should be of tried integrity and patriotism, of great courage and bodily endurance, and known ability; and a

The Farmer Boy and How He Became Commander-in-Chief

resident of some central province, that in him might be blended the extreme interests of North and South, which would tend to lessen the jealousies of the two sections, and harmonize them, as it were, into one. Such a province was Virginia, and such a man was Col. Washington; whom, therefore, he commended to the favor and consideration of the Honorable House.

Before this address was ended, Washington, perceiving that he was the person on the point of being singled out, rose from his seat, much agitated and embarrassed, and hastily quitted the House.

Next morning, Mr. Adams's recommendation was acted upon; and the House, without a single dissenting voice, chose GEORGE WASHINGTON to be *Commander-in-chief* of all the army of the United Colonies, with the salary of six thousand dollars a year. In his reply, Washington expressed his grateful sense of so signal a proof of the confidence reposed in him by his countrymen, and added, —

"But lest some unfortunate event should happen, unfavorable to my reputation, I beg that it may be remembered by every gentleman in this room, that I this day declare, with the utmost sincerity, that I do not think myself equal to the command I am honored with. As to pay, I beg leave to assure the Congress, that, as no pecuniary consideration could have tempted me to accept of this employment at the expense of my domestic ease and happiness, I do not wish to make any profit of it. I will keep an exact account of my expenses: these, I doubt not, they will discharge; and that is all I desire."

In a letter to Mrs. Washington, informing her of the great change thus made in his destiny, he deplores the hard necessity that makes it his duty to give up the sweet pleasures of home and her society; and exhorts her, in affectionate language, to bear up under their separation with cheerfulness and fortitude; at the same time giving her the gratifying assurance, that with her he could have more happiness at Mount Vernon in one month, than he could hope to find without her, were he to remain abroad seven times seven years. From the tone of this letter, she must readily have guessed that the place was not one of his own seeking.

The Farmer Boy and How He Became Commander-in-Chief

Accordingly, on the 21st of June, General Washington,—for so we must now call him,—having received his commission, set out to take command of the American army, then lying before Boston, which, being occupied by the king's troops, was in a state of siege. A company of Pennsylvania light-horse escorted him from Philadelphia to New York, where he was received with all the honor due, not only to the high station he had been called to fill, but also to his exalted character and distinguished abilities. Here he heard further particulars of the battle of Bunker's Hill, fought near Boston a few days before. From New York, the general-in-chief proceeded to Boston, and was greeted everywhere on the way with the greatest enthusiasm by the people, who came streaming in from all quarters to behold the man into whose keeping had been intrusted the destinies of America.

Thus, my dear children, I have brought you, step by step, up to that great event in Washington's life when his character and actions were to be subjected to the gaze and scrutiny, not only of his own age and country, but of all ages to come, and of all the nations of Christendom.

XXVI.

CONCLUSION.

Here Uncle Juvinell paused, and, with a countenance of undisturbed sobriety, emptied his ninth mug. In justice, however, to the good man, this pattern of old-fashioned gentility, it must be borne in mind, that the mug was a Dutch mug, and consequently a small one (as indeed are all things Dutch, from clocks to cheeses); and also that, small as it was, he never more than half filled it, except once or twice in the course of an evening, when he would gird up his loins, as it were, with a brimmer to help him over some passage in his story of unusual knottiness and difficulty.

Willie (whose surname should have been fox or weasel or lynx), having heretofore divided his attention between what his uncle imparted and what he imbibed, had, by careful counting, discovered that the ninth mug invariably closed their evening lessons: so, without waiting for any further signal that such was now the case, he alertly bounced from his chair, and, snatching up a basket of big red apples that black daddy had just brought in and set on the hearth, began handing them round to the rest of the company with a great show of playing the polite and obliging, but taking care, when unobserved, to pick out the largest and mellowest one of them all for himself, and smuggle it under his coat-tail. When all were helped, he reset the basket on the hearth, and with a grand flourish, unmasking his royal red, opened wide his mouth, as if he would have bolted it whole: but, seeming to think better of it, he carefully laid it in Uncle Juvinell's mug, which it exactly filled, saying as he did so, "It goes to my heart to part with you; but only the king of historians is worthy to enjoy the queen of apples." Then, plunging his hand into the basket, he snatched up another, hap-hazard, and began eating it with savage voracity, as if made reckless by this act of self-denial. Re-seating himself as he had chosen his apple, hap-hazard, he missed his chair, and keeled over, bringing his heels in the air where his head should have been, and his head on the rug where the dog and cat were, and the half-munched plug in his mouth, plump into his windpipe, so as to almost strangle him out of his breeches, and cause his buttons to fly like grains from a corn-cob when thrown into a corn-sheller. Of course, all the little folks fairly screamed with laughter, in which even Uncle Juvinell could not help joining right heartily: nor would he venture upon the broad wedge which he had cut out of his apple, till his chuckle was well ended; when he remarked, that "Willie was one of the boys we read about." To which Willie, picking himself up again, replied, that "he rather thought he was not, just then, but perhaps would be as soon as he could get back some of the breath he had lost, and gather up the buttons he had shed." Then, drawing down his waistcoat from under his arm-pits to hide a breadth of white muslin not usually intended for the eyes of a mixed company, he reseated himself with such care and circumspection, that the middle seam of his breeches tallied exactly with the middle round of the chair-back, and began mincing and nibbling his apple delicately like a sheep, as if to show that he meant to profit by the lesson his fit of strangling had taught him.

After a little while, when he saw that the children had had their fill of laughter and red apples, Uncle Juvinell wiped the blade of his knife with his bandanna, and said, "And now, my darlings, don't you think we are getting along swimmingly?"

"Swimmingly!" they all chimed in with one voice.

"Gloriously?" again inquired Uncle Juvinell.

"Gloriously!" cried all the children at once, as pat to their uncle's words as an echo to the sound. Whereupon the old gentleman's spectacles shone with a lustre that was charming to see. In a moment after, however, Bryce, the pugnacious urchin of ten, expressed himself a little disappointed that they had had so much building of forts, and digging and cutting of roads, and so much scouting and marching, and so much getting ready to fight, and yet withal so little downright fighting.

"You quite forget, Bryce, that affair of Grant's defeat there at Fort Duquesne," said Willie. "In my opinion, that was a very decent, respectable piece of bloodshed; and quite as good as Braddock's disaster, as far as it goes."

"How heartless you must be, Willie, to speak so lightly of such horrible things!" exclaimed Miss Laura with a look of refined disgust. "To my mind, Washington's courtship and wedding, and the pleasant life he led at Mount Vernon, are more entertaining than all your dismal battles."

"And those charming barge-rides by moonlight," chimed in Ella, "that the old Virginia planters used to take when they visited each other up and down the Potomac."

"You are welcome to your courtships and your weddings and your boat-rides by moonlight," cried Willie, turning up his nose; "but I would not have given a good fox-hunt with old Lord Fairfax for any of them: and what a glorious fellow Washington must have been, with his fine horses and his fine dogs, and his jumping twenty-one feet seven inches at a bound!"

"Oh, Willie! how can you be so wanting in respect as to call such a man as Washington *'fellow'*?" exclaimed Laura, with a look of pious horror. "I am astonished at you!"

"But I said he was glorious; didn't I now, Miss Over-nice?" retorted Willie.

"Your Cousin Laura, William, is quite right in what she says," observed Uncle Juvinell, with something like severity in his look and tone. "We should never speak of the good and great in other terms than those of esteem and reverence; for the effect of such a habit is to cultivate in ourselves those very qualities of mind and heart which make them worthy of our love and admiration."

Willie was somewhat abashed by this mild rebuke, and apologized in a dumb way by coughing a time or two behind his slate.

"Uncle," inquired Ella, "is transcendentalism an art or a science?"

"I think I can tell you what that is, Ella," Daniel made haste to put in; for he never let an opportunity slip of showing off what he knew to the best advantage.

"I did not call upon you for information, Mr. Wiseacre," said Ella, a little nettled at her brother's air of superior wisdom.

"Nevertheless," cried Uncle Juvinell, "let us listen, and be wise. Come, give us the benefit of your knowledge, Daniel, touching this important matter."

"I overheard father say to you the other day," replied Daniel, without hesitation, "that your transcendentalism, uncle, was an equal mixture of opium, moonshine, fog, and sick-man's dreams."

"Good! you have hit it exactly!" cried Uncle Juvinell; "and, to reward you for your diligence in picking up and storing away such precious bits of knowledge, I promise you for your next Christmas present a gilt-edged copy of Bunyan's 'Pilgrim's Progress.'"

"I thank you very much, dear uncle," replied Dannie; "but, if it makes no difference with you, I would prefer 'Josephus' to 'Bunyan.'"

"Certainly, certainly, my dear nephew; it shall be as you wish," replied Uncle Juvinell, a little provoked with himself for having been so thoughtless as to overlook the fact, that Daniel, being a curly-headed, Jewish boy, was not likely to be much interested in the ups and downs of good old Christian's doleful pilgrimage.

"Tell me, uncle," cried John, who had an ear for rhyme, "what is meant by taxation, and legislation by representation, in a nation. Is it sense, or only poetry?"

"Bad poetry, but mighty good sense, my little boy," replied Uncle Juvinell; "and, if you will be right attentive, I will endeavor to make clear to you what is meant thereby. In a popular form of government,—such as the one we live under,—the people tax themselves, and make laws for themselves, through persons chosen by themselves, and from among themselves, to serve for a certain term of months or years in our State Legislatures or in our National Congress, as the case may be. The persons whom the people thus authorize to tax them and make laws, or, as it is otherwise termed, to legislate for them, representing, as they do, the will, desires, and wants of the communities by whom they are chosen, are called representatives; and hence the phrase, 'taxation, and representation by legislation.'"

"In a nation," added Johnnie, by way of giving it a finish, and to show that it was all as clear as day to him.

"Yes, in a nation and a state too," rejoined Uncle Juvinell, with a merry twinkle in his eye.

"Will you have the kindness, uncle," said Dannie, "to tell us the difference between a legislature and a congress and a parliament?"

"In our own country," replied Uncle Juvinell, "a legislature is the law-making assembly of a State, and Congress is the law-making assembly of the whole nation; while Parliament is the great law-making or legislative assembly of Great Britain and Ireland. The rules and regulations in all these bodies are quite similar; and, besides being vested with the power of laying taxes and making laws, they perform other services necessary to the safety and welfare of the state or nation. Thus the old Continental Congress was composed of representatives from all the thirteen States, which entitled each, through its representation, to one vote, and to equal weight and influence with the rest, in the acts and deliberations of this assembly, no matter what may have been its size and population, whether large or small; nor what the number of its representatives, whether one or several."

"And will you also tell me, uncle, wherein a convention differs from all these legislative assemblies?" said Daniel, grappling manfully with the tall words, but staggering under them nevertheless.

"Simply not being legislative at all, as the term is now generally used in our country," replied Uncle Juvinell. "A convention is a body of men assembled together as representatives of a party or state or nation, for some special purpose, such as the formation of a new State Constitution, or for making changes in an old one, or to give expression to the views and designs of a party, and to nominate candidates to the various offices of the government; which purpose being effected, they are dissolved, and cease to exist or to have any legal force."

The Farmer Boy and How He Became Commander-in-Chief

"And why, uncle, was the name 'Continental' given to our first Congress?" inquired Willie.

"To distinguish it from the Congress of the several States, and as the one in which the common interest and welfare of all the States of the continent were represented," was Uncle Juvinell's reply; and then he added, "And hence the same term was applied to whatever belonged to the States conjointly, and grew out of their union or confederation. Thus, for example, besides the Continental Congress, there was a Continental Army, raised, equipped, and supported at the joint expense of all the States, and subject in a great measure to the control of the Continental Congress. And there was the Continental uniform, which was the uniform worn by an officer or a soldier of the Continental Army. And there was the Continental currency, which was the paper-money issued and put into circulation by the Continental Congress, all the States unitedly holding themselves accountable for its redemption in specie; or, in other words, binding themselves, after having gained their independence as a nation, to take it back at the value specified thereon, and giving to those who held it gold and silver in exchange. But more of this in another place."

"And what is a minister, uncle?" inquired Laura. "And what is a commissioner, uncle?" chimed in Ella. "And what is a revenue, uncle?" put in Charlie. "And what is a remonstrance, uncle?" inquired Bryce, following up the attack.

"Hold, you rogues! and one at a time!" cried Uncle Juvinell. "A minister, Laura, in the sense in which we have been using the term, is a high officer of State, intrusted with the control and management of some office or department of the national government, such as that of the navy or war or treasury or commerce or foreign affairs. All the ministers, taken collectively, make up what is called the ministry; who, besides discharging the duties of their respective offices, are also expected to serve as counsellors to the king, and aid him in carrying out the measures of the government. A commissioner, Ella, is an agent appointed and authorized by another, or a number of others, or a State, to transact some business of a private or public character, as the case may be. A revenue,

The Farmer Boy and How He Became Commander-in-Chief

Charlie, is the income or yearly sum of money of a State, raised from taxes on the people or their property, from duties on foreign merchandise imported into the country, and from the sale of public lands and other sources, to meet the expenses of the government. A remonstrance, Bryce, is a setting-forth in strong terms, either by writing or by word of mouth, the facts and reasons against something complained of or opposed, as unjust, unwise, or unadvisable."

"I can't imagine," said Daniel, with the air of one who had weighed well in his own mind a matter of importance, "what advantage to themselves or to the nation George the Third and his ministers could have expected, when they laid those heavy taxes on their American Colonies, then took from them the power to pay them by crippling their commerce and putting a stop to their manufactures; and it seems strange to me that Englishmen could ever have denied to Englishmen the rights and liberties of Englishmen, without having something more to gain." Here Daniel broke down, and scratched his head; and Uncle Juvinell, with an approving, good-humored smile, replied, "Those very questions, Daniel, have puzzled many an older head than yours, and many a wiser head than mine; and, indeed, some of the most learned historians, who have written about these matters, have expressed themselves perplexed at this strange conduct of the king and his ministers, and have been able to account for it only on the supposition, that they were all, for the time being, bereft of their wits, and therefore rendered incapable of foreseeing the tremendous consequences of their unjust and ill-judged measures."

Much gratified at the interest the little folks had taken in such dry matters, and seeing that they had no more questions to put to him, and that some of the smaller ones were already nodding in their chairs, Uncle Juvinell, by way of winding up the evening's entertainment, concluded thus:—

"Some of you, my dear children, have read how good Christian, in his pilgrimage to the Celestial City, went on sometimes sighingly, sometimes comfortably, until he came to the foot of a hill called Difficulty, where he found three roads to choose between. The one to the right went around the bottom of the hill, and led into a wilderness of dark woods, out of which no one ever found his way again after venturing therein. The one to the left went likewise around the bottom of the hill, and led into a wilderness of dark mountains, which was even more difficult to escape from than the one to the right. But the middle road, which was narrow and straight, went right up the steep and flinty sides of the hill, and was the route that led direct to Mount Zion. Not being the man to flinch from any difficulty, however great, good Christian hesitated not a moment to choose the middle road; and accordingly he fell from running to walking, and from walking to going, and from going to clambering upon his hands and knees, till he had made his way to the top. Here, as you must well remember, there met his view a stately palace called Beautiful, kept by a company of prim, precise, proper, prudent, and pious maiden ladies, who gave our weary pilgrim a cordial but well-considered reception, and, besides admitting him to the hospitalities of the house gratis, entertained him with a variety of pleasing and edifying discourse. And you have not forgotten, either, how, when they had a clear morning, these discreet and well-ordered damsels, to reward him for the zeal and diligence with which he had heretofore pursued his journey, as well as to encourage him to still further effort, led him up to the top of their house, whence he might have a delightful view of the Delectable Mountains, far, far away. And you also still hear in mind, how poor Christian must needs pass through the dismal Vale of Humiliation, and there meet in deadly fight the terrible monster Apollyon; then through the Valley and Shadow of Death, with all its doleful sights and sounds; then through the wicked city of Vanity Fair; then through the gloomy domains of Doubting Castle and Giant Despair,—all before he could hope to set foot on these Delectable Mountains of Emanuel's land.

"Now, do you not see, my dear children, that not altogether unlike good Christian's case, at this stage of his journey, is that of our own at this point of our story? But a little while ago we were trudging along, sometimes heavily, sometimes swimmingly, till by and by we reached the bottom of our Hill Difficulty; by which, of course, you understand me to mean the causes that brought about our Revolutionary War. And here, had we gone to the right or the left, we should most assuredly have wandered into a wilderness of romance and Brobdignagian wonders, among whose mazes we would have become entangled beyond all reasonable hope of escape. But our eyes were opened to our danger; and like good Christian, by whose example we might profit oftener than we do, we knew in what direction lay our best interest, and were not to be enticed astray by the prospect of ease or novelty, nor turned back by flinty facts and rough realities. So straightway up the difficult hill we marched, lofty and steep as it was; and hardly left a stone unturned till we had scrambled to the top. This gained, we have felt it our privilege to halt and rest a while, and refresh ourselves with a little pleasing and edifying discourse, one with another, touching what we have seen or heard in the course of our journey.

"We have thus surmounted the most tedious and difficult part of our story. But still there lies before us many a hard-fought battle, many an irksome siege, many a forlorn retreat, many a gloomy winter-camp, and many a season of doubt and discouragement, privation and dire calamity, through which we must pass before we can hope to set our weary feet on the Delectable Mountains of Freemen's Land, smiling invitingly beyond. But to reward you for the diligent attention with which you have followed me thus far, as well as to entice you to trudge on to the end, I will, from this elevated point, unfold to your view a glimpse of this glorious region, ere 'the war-clouds rolling dun' from the plains of Lexington and the heights of Bunker's Hill have too much obscured our morning sky.

"See yon land of shining mountains,
   Stately forests, verdant dells,
Sun-bright rivers, sparkling fountains,
   Healthful breezes, balmy smells,
Golden grain-fields, pleasant meadows,
   Fruitful orchards, gardens fair,
Lasting sunshine, fleeting shadows!
   Freedom dwells for ever there!
Hark! what song is that high swelling,
   Like an anthem dropped from heaven,
Of some joyful tidings telling,
   Some rich boon to mankind given?

The Farmer Boy and How He Became Commander-in-Chief

'Tis a happy people, singing
   Thanks for Freedom's victory won;
Valley, forest, mountain, ringing
   With one name,—great Washington.
Through distress, through tribulation,
   Through the lowering clouds of war,
They have risen to be a nation:
   Freedom shines, their morning-star.
Would we reach those realms of glory,
   Would we join that righteous band,
We must speed us in our story:
   Come, let's on to Freemen's Land!"

The next evening, the little folks, upon repairing to the library, found their Uncle Juvinell seated, as was his wont, cross-legged in his great arm-chair, looking with a fixed and absent gaze into 'the glowing embers of the fire,' as if his thoughts were far away.

In his hand he held an open letter which he had just brought from the post-office, in the contents whereof, it was evident, he had found somewhat of a painful character; for a slight shadow had dimmed the brightness of his otherwise placid countenance. So rare a thing as that of a cloud on their good old uncle's sunny face caught their notice at once; and instead of gathering round him in their usual coaxing, teasing, bantering, frolicsome way, they seated themselves quietly on either hand, and awaited in respectful silence until he should rise to the surface of the deep brown-study into which he seemed to be plunged. But the longer he sat, the harder he looked at the fire, and the deeper he sank into his revery, till the little folks began to fear that it would be a full hour before he would reach the bottom and come up again.

Daniel, the young historian, sat watching his uncle's countenance with his sharp black eyes, expecting each moment to hear him break the silence with, "After the battle of Bunker's Hill;" or, "Washington, upon his arrival at Boston;" or something to that effect. But, last in his own thoughts, Uncle Juvinell still sat cross-legged in his arm-chair, and spoke not a word. At last, just by way of reminding him that a select and highly enlightened audience were in waiting to hear

The Farmer Boy and How He Became Commander-in-Chief

him, Willie softly arose from his chair, and, filling the little Dutch mug to the brim with rich brown cider, offered it to his uncle, with a forward duck of the head and a backward jerk of the heel, which he, no doubt, intended for a genteel bow. Uncle Juvinell took it; but set it again, with an absent air, untasted on the table. Then, drawing his spectacles down from his forehead, he again perused the letter he held in his hand, with earnest attention, the shadow on his brow deepening as he read.

When he had finished, he laid it on the table, and finally broke the long silence; his first words falling like ice-water on the ears of the little folks.

"Sad news for you, my dear children; sad news for us all! I have just received a letter from my old friend and kinsman, Peter Parley, of whom you have all heard so much, and to whom, for the many delightful books he has written, the younger generations of America are more indebted than perhaps to any man now living. In his letter he tells me, that, owing to his declining health, and increasing years, he has ceased his literary labors altogether, and betaken himself to New Orleans, in whose milder climate he hopes he may, in some measure, recruit his failing powers. What he says in addition to this I will give you in his own words:—

"The effects of that unlucky fall on the ice, while crossing Boston Common, so many years ago, I have felt in my right hip, to a greater or less degree, ever since; and within the past year my lameness has so much increased as to have become a matter of much anxiety to my friends, and some uneasiness to myself. Taking this in connection with the growing infirmities of age, I sometimes have a foreboding that I shall never return to Boston alive.

"Under this impression, I now write you, my Cousin Juvinell, entreating you, as my nearest living kinsman and much-beloved friend, to come and see me at this place, and sojourn here with me, until, in the wisdom of a kind Providence, it be determined whether my span of life is to be shortened or lengthened yet a little more. It will be a comfort to me to have you by my side at the closing scene; and it may be that your cheerful presence and sunny humor will do more to revive me than I can hope for even from this mild, pleasant Louisiana air.

"I know that your compliance with my request will for a season prove a serious interruption to the enjoyment of the little folks in your vicinity, whom you have taken under your wing, and to whose entertainment and instruction so much of your useful life is devoted. But they will, I am sure, without hesitation, make this sacrifice in behalf of one who has for many long years labored so hard and faithfully for their happiness and improvement. Commend me kindly to them. Hoping to see you at an early day, I remain, as ever, your affectionate friend and kinsman,

"PETER PARLEY."

Uncle Juvinell went on: "I am gratified, my dear children, to see in your grateful and sympathetic looks, saddened and disappointed though I know you really to be, that you are ready and willing to sacrifice what pleasure and entertainment my company and conversation may afford you, to the comfort and wishes of this venerated and excellent man. My going-away at this moment will, it is true, cause a sad interruption to our story of the life of Washington; but next Christmas, if we all be spared, and your Uncle Juvinell keep his memory fresh and green, we will gather together again in this very room, and take it up where we now drop it, and follow it through all its eventful changes to the glorious and happy end. Meanwhile, ponder well in your minds what I have already told you of the childhood, youth, and early prime of this illustrious man. And after all, now that I give the matter a second thought, we could not have been interrupted at a more suitable place; for the account I have given up to this point needs scarcely a single important particular to make it a complete and separate story. We have followed him step by step, and seen how he rose, first from the boy-farmer to the youthful surveyor, from that to the young colonel, from that to the legislator of more mature years, and lastly from that to commander-in-chief of the armies of a young and rising nation.

"The history of his career after this period is, in fact, so closely connected with that of his country, as to be altogether inseparable from it.

"And again I repeat, ponder well in your minds what I have already told you, as being, after all, the part most necessary for you at present to know. Ever strive to keep his example before your eyes, ever to cherish his virtues in your hearts. Like him, be industrious in your habits, diligent in your studies, polite in your manners, orderly in your dress, peaceable in your disposition, upright in your dealings, faithful in your friendships, patient under trials, persevering under difficulties, strangers to covetousness, content with little, moderate with much, generous, self-denying, courageous in well-doing, pure in heart, devout in spirit, modest before men, reverent to your parents, respectful to your superiors, humble before God; and, like him, let the clear light of truth shine forth in all your words, in all your actions, in all your looks and gestures, in all your secret thoughts, and in your very souls. Be all this, that men may reverence you, that angels may honor you, that God may bless and reward you."

Here Uncle Juvinell paused; and, as he looked round on the saddened faces of his little auditors, a moisture crept out softly upon his eyelashes, and dimmed the brightness of his spectacles. "It grieves me much, my dearest children," said he, after a moment or two,—and there was a tremor of deep fatherly feeling in his voice,—"it grieves me much, that our happy little circle must be broken up. It will be but for a season, however; and, when we meet again, we shall be happier than had we not parted at all. On Monday, I take the stage-coach for Louisville; and there I take the steamer 'Eclipse' for New Orleans. As it is a long journey I have before me, I must needs write many letters, and do a deal of packing, before setting out: so we will sing our evening hymn now, and separate for the night."

Then, joining their voices together, they sang that beautiful hymn, "Though far away from friends and home." At the second line, however,—"A lonely wanderer I may roam,"—the little folks fairly broke down; their hearts rising into their throats from very grief, and choking their voices: but, with all the ease of a professed singing-master, Uncle Juvinell, though his heart was full too, glided at once from the lowest bass to the highest treble, which he carried alone, until some of the children, getting the better of their feelings, chimed in with him, when he softly dropped to the very bottom of his bass again.

The hymn ended, the little folks came one by one, and, without speaking a word, embraced and kissed their dear old uncle, this best of men; he laying his gentle hand upon their bowed heads, and blessing them with more than his usual fervor.

THE END.